Managing Elevated Risk

Iwan J. Azis · Hyun Song Shin

Managing Elevated Risk

Global Liquidity, Capital Flows, and Macroprudential Policy—An Asian Perspective

ADB

Springer Open

ISBN 978-981-10-1379-9 ISBN 978-981-287-284-5 (eBook)
DOI 10.1007/978-981-287-284-5

Softcover reprint of the hardcover 1st edition 2015

Note:
In this publication, "$" refers to US dollars.

Printed on recycled paper

Foreword

The frequent financial crises in the 1990s and the culminating 2008/2009 global recession have had worldwide impact. They have become less and less regional and more global. Increasingly important when defining their impact, however, are the policy responses taken. These have changed the nature and intensity of global liquidity, particularly when crisis and response originated in the world's largest economy.

Loose monetary policy in the United States during the early 2000s marked the beginning of major changes in global liquidity. These significantly affected emerging economies—especially in Asia. But nothing was more dramatic than the impact of the policy response to the global financial crisis. Consequently, concerns over financial instability mounted. This dramatic effect on global liquidity warrants a new regulatory framework, alternative early warning indicators, and—as a result—a set of macroprudential policies to complement standard monetary policy.

Before the 2008/2009 crisis, the predominant thinking centered around the lack of preconditions for successful financial liberalization. Corruption, weak enforcement, and limited understanding about how a liberalized financial sector operates were to blame. Recommendations thus focused on fixing those institutional factors—rather than questioning the virtue of the frictionless capital flows under capital account liberalization policy. Only after crisis struck the United States and Europe—where these institutional factors were supposedly strong—did people begin to challenge the predominant view and attention switched to financial regulation.

But the regulations proposed could also seriously impact other economies. If the "voice" of non-crisis economies—which includes most of emerging Asia—is not adequately heard, the new regulations could be disproportionally hard and unnecessarily harsh. Unless this financial regulatory asymmetry is corrected by listening to what emerging markets have to say, there is the risk that proposed regulations will lose their effectiveness. This is where the analysis in *Managing Elevated Risks* is useful.

Sponsored by the Asian Development Bank (ADB), the study was initiated in 2011 to look at three main issues: (i) how Asian economies translate the lessons of the global financial crisis into appropriate policies and reforms in terms of macro-prudential supervision relative to micro-prudential supervision; (ii) how robust are financial sector policies or reforms as a buffer to any systemic vulnerability to financial crises, and the extent of their contribution to financial soundness and stability; and (iii) what strategic direction should financial policies and regulatory reforms take. Three conferences were held—an inception seminar in July 2012 at ADB headquarters; a January 2013 meeting at the Hong Kong Monetary Authority with over 60 representatives of regulatory agencies, the private sector and academe; and a July 2013 conference in Seoul, Republic of Korea to discuss the results of research conducted on financial regulatory reform. Regulators from across Asia and the Pacific attended this final event.

Managing Elevated Risks is ultimately about how changes in global liquidity affect emerging Asia. It is intended to raise our understanding about the warranted regulatory framework and alternative early warning indicators—and from this to provide guidance in formulating a set of appropriate macroprudential policies. It highlights the mechanisms of how massive capital flows through noncore bank liabilities and capital markets can elevate the risk of financial instability and worsening socio-economic conditions, limiting the effectiveness of standard monetary policy.

This book would not have been completed without the excellent support from Raquel Borres, Marthe Hinojales, and Jong-Ho Lee of the ADB. The authors thank them for having helped bring the book to publication, and particularly for Ms. Hinojales, who co-authored Chap. 4, for her excellent research assistance.

Contents

Chapter 1
Introduction and Overview

After the 1997/1998 Asian financial crisis, many economies in the region set out to rebuild their savings, sometimes to excess. Capital inflows further boosted liquidity after interest rates in the US and Europe fell in early 2000. The resulting combination of large savings and lower borrowing costs spurred credit creation and economic growth, especially in emerging Asia. At the same time, appreciation pressures on exchange rates increased as did the overall risk to financial stability. Procyclicality risks are particularly high when capital flows reverse direction: Rapid liquidity growth can turn into a sharp contraction. So with plenty of liquidity and low borrowing costs, individuals, banks, and companies all shifted their preference toward more risky investments.

What started this trend? The 2000s began with easy money policies in advanced economies. Responding to the 2000 recession and the 11 September 2001 political shock, the US federal funds rate fell precipitously—from over 6 % in 2001 to just 1 % by the summer of 2003. Over the same period, the European Central Bank (ECB) rate dropped from over 4 to 2 %. Fears of asset bubbles subsequently brought interest rates back up in the US and Europe. By late 2007, on the eve of recession and the subprime crisis, rates had risen fivefold in the US and doubled in Europe. As the US recession began in December 2007, the US Federal Reserve (US Fed) shifted gears again, lowering rates steadily—from more than 5 to 2 % by mid-2008. The subsequent collapse of Lehman Brothers in September that year forced the US Fed to be more aggressive. Rates fell to 0.25 % and remained there, at least through the third quarter of 2014 (when this was written). Interest rates in the Eurozone fell just as dramatically—a steady decline from over 4 % in 2007 to 1 % shortly after the Lehman crisis, to 0.5 % in mid-2013, and 0.15 % currently.

Global liquidity responded accordingly. Massive amounts of capital surged out of advanced economies into emerging markets. Emerging Asia was among the biggest beneficiaries—estimated inflows between November 2008 and April 2013

I.J. Azis and H.S. Shin, *Managing Elevated Risk*,
DOI 10.1007/978-981-287-284-5_1

totaled $2.1 trillion. Early on, much of these inflows were intermediated through banks (throughout this book called "bank-led flows"). This was the first phase of global liquidity. Then, in 2008, the worst crisis since the 1930s Great Depression erupted. Capital flows plunged worldwide, but rapidly recovered. By autumn 2010, liquidity flows were surging again, although this time predominantly through capital markets, including local currency bond markets (called "debt-led flows" here). This was the second phase of global liquidity. Compared with what led to the 1997/1998 Asian financial crisis, the size of flows going to emerging Asia was larger and more volatile. If reversed, the impact would be quickly felt. For example, when the US Fed announced in May 2013 its intention to taper quantitative easing (QE), investors quickly pulled out of emerging markets. Some markets were clearly rattled, hitting affected economies with a double-punch—volatile capital markets and depreciated exchange rates. With the knowledge US monetary policy would soon begin to "normalize," risk perceptions toward emerging markets rose. Those with perceived vulnerabilities saw the greatest volatility. This is what we call the third phase of global liquidity.

This book describes these three phases of global liquidity and their impact on emerging Asia from conceptual and empirical perspectives. What stands out is the important role noncore bank liabilities played in the process. Together with the growing significance of capital markets in the second phase, it has changed the financial and monetary policy landscape sufficiently to warrant a new regulatory framework, alternative early warning indicators, and as a result a set of macroprudential policies to complement monetary policy.

After discussing conceptual and measurement issues related to this changing global liquidity, Chap. 2 presents the background and details of how global liquidity evolved from phase one to phase two and then phase three.

Permissive conditions in the US dollar wholesale market were behind the development of phase one—with liquidity transmitted via the global banking system to the rest of the world, including emerging Asia. This showed up in expanding bank balance sheets through increased noncore liabilities that facilitated more and larger lending, along with greater risk-taking behavior. Even nonfinancial institutions took on attributes of financial firms ("financialization"), as they increased the size of their balance sheets relative to generating sales. As a consequence, this contributed to the amplification of financial cycles. Currency appreciation further fueled inflows as borrowers' balance sheets were strengthened. To the extent rising noncore liabilities are highly procyclical and are an important transmission channel of global liquidity shocks to emerging Asia, the resulting financial cycles were out of sync with domestic business cycles. As a result, on top of the elevated risks caused by the bank-led credit boom, it also reduced the effectiveness of monetary policy—and this led to the call for separate macroprudential policy.

In phase two, the massive amount of inflows into emerging markets saw credit grow through corporate bond issuance by nonfinancial borrowers. In emerging Asia, governments used the opportunity of low-cost financing to increase their bond issuance, allowing them to make "maturity adjustments" (sovereign bonds replacing short-term debt). The region's capital markets boomed during this phase. Local currency bonds outstanding reached $7.2 trillion by March 2014, a dramatic increase considering that some economies in the region had virtually no bond market prior to 1997. Also, the share of foreign ownership in local currency bond markets rose, as did bank holdings of sovereign bonds. With interest rates low, the issuance of international government and corporate securities in emerging markets also increased rapidly. If the vulnerability in the first phase caused by bank-led flows through noncore liabilities is linked with procyclicality effects, the second phase vulnerability caused by debt-led flows is associated with sporadic and sudden outflows.

The first and second phases of global liquidity set the stage for the third phase. Here, the story is about capital flow reversals. The bond market sell-off following the hint that QE would soon begin tapering in mid-2013 spread quickly to emerging markets, with an immediate impact of rising bond yields, higher interbank rates, and depreciating currencies, albeit not evenly across all markets. With banks holding large amounts of securities and equities, the link between banks and capital markets is strong. Any shock that causes asset prices to fall can worsen bank balance sheets. This complicates policy choices, especially in economies where the local investor base is small and macrofundamentals weak.

But even economies with relatively good fundamentals saw capital exit, as US market risk was perceived to be lower. All of these economies saw their exchange rates depreciate against the US dollar, with the exception of the renminbi and Philippine peso. Bond markets in economies with strong fundamentals (such as Malaysia; the Philippines; Hong Kong, China; and Singapore) also saw bond yields rise. Typically prone to "buying the rumor and selling the news," their respective equity markets also suffered.

Given the different circumstances of each phase, Chap. 3 argues that relevant early warning indicators should also evolve and be adjusted based on the main drivers of inflows and associated risks. In phase one, banks are center stage in credit growth, a focus on noncore liabilities of financial intermediaries will most likely yield timely signals. On the other hand, when spending and credit are funded by bond issuance in phase two, an appropriate early warning indicator would emphasize aggregate issuance. Tracking aggregate corporate cash holdings is also important to mitigate risks caused by "carry trade" activities. The bulk of the discussion in Chap. 3 is devoted to this. For phase three, the challenge is more complex. But as the stage was set by the first and second phases, the indicators proposed in phase one and phase two remain relevant for phase three.

Chapter 4 scrutinizes the extent to which emerging Asia's noncore liabilities have reached a level that makes them vulnerable. Although Asia's share of noncore liabilities in total liabilities remains relatively small, they have grown rapidly as a ratio to GDP. Consistent with findings based on the Flow of Fund analysis cited in Chap. 2, we show the increase significantly contributed to the expansion of bank assets. The important contribution of noncore liabilities to credit growth is also confirmed by the regression test we conducted, supporting our conjecture that a relevant early warning indicator should focus on noncore liabilities. More importantly, it limits the effectiveness of monetary policy. And if this limitation is overlooked—existing monetary policy intensified by adding more—the probability of bank bankruptcies would increase as a bank's net worth tends to decline. Hence, an effective macroprudential policy that supplements standard monetary policy is needed to make monetary policy more effective, with financial stability added as an additional objective.

The extent that changes in global liquidity combine with a liberalized financial sector enhances the amount of liquidity flowing in. But it also increases the risk of instability. Thus, it would have helped had there been more global and regional cooperation in policymaking. In reality, however, even as economies become more interdependent, national policy continues to rule irrespective of spillovers on other economies and all the talk of cooperation and policy coordination. The ultra-easy monetary policies adopted in advanced economies ("financial nationalism") are a case in point. In turn, this forces policy makers in emerging markets to take unilateral policies to mitigate the resulting impact.

While the focus of the discussion so far has been on the implications of capital flows on financial and macroeconomic stability, their impact on development must be assessed. This is done in Chap. 5. By using a general equilibrium framework with a rather detailed financial module, we show that capital inflows are closely linked to income inequality. We argue that capital inflows not only increase the risk of financial instability, but also the inequality in household income distribution—particularly if banks with the new liquidity take on more risky investments. On the other hand, results of model simulations show that when banks act prudently by allocating loans to more productive investments in the real economy—rather than parking funds in risky financial instruments—capital inflows would improve income inequality. This is because output grows, and hence, the increase in factor income is higher than the increase in financial income accrued by retail investors from rich urban households. Therefore, the challenge is how to create a system where banks are discouraged from taking on risky investments. From this perspective, macroprudential policy would also work toward reducing income inequality in the case of rising capital inflows.

Typically, income inequality is never explicitly on the list of criteria for designing macro and financial policy. Yet inequality is rising in nearly all economies—advanced and emerging alike—and increasingly tops the development challenges faced by policymakers. How would adding another objective alter the priority of policy alternatives? Would adding the social goal of reducing income inequality change policy choices? And, in particular, would macroprudential policy remain relevant? We cite the benefits and advantage of imposing a levy on noncore liabilities as one potential macroprudential policy. How well would this work compared with other policies? Based on a perception model, the analysis in the final section of Chap. 5 shows the answer depends on whether or not we consider both upsides and downsides of each policy alternative. Encouraging capital outflows during tranquil periods—rather than assigning a levy to noncore liabilities—works better when only policy benefits are considered. But when the costs and risks are taken into account simultaneously with the benefits, assigning a levy on noncore liabilities makes better sense.

Thus, while this book argues throughout that in the midst of changing global liquidity macroprudential policy is needed to complement monetary policy, the analysis in Chap. 5 shows that certain type of macroprudential policy can also be favorable for reducing income inequality.

As there are many ways to group macroprudential tools, Chap. 6 classifies those tools by distinguishing between (i) asset-side tools that directly limit bank loan growth; (ii) liability-side tools that limit vulnerability to liquidity and currency mismatches; and (iii) bank capital-oriented tools that limit loan growth through altering bank incentives. Assigning a levy on noncore liabilities is among the liability-side tools we propose to address the buildup of vulnerabilities to liquidity and currency mismatches and the underpricing of global capital market risk. It mitigates pricing distortions that lead to excessive asset growth. The Financial Stability Contribution (FSC) recommended by the International Monetary Fund (IMF) on the bank levy to the G20 leaders in June 2010 is an example of such a corrective tax. We believe the levy could mitigate the buildup of systemic risk through currency or maturity mismatches by counteracting distortions to global funding conditions and the "supply push" from global banks.

So the main message is this: The dynamics of global liquidity since early 2000 has had ramifications worldwide, the most important a surge in capital flows. For emerging markets on the receiving end—which includes those in Asia—liquidity surged, first through banks' increased noncore liabilities and then via expanding capital markets. Both boosted investment and growth. But at the same time, they also elevated the risk of instability, worsened income inequality, and reduced the effectiveness of monetary policy. Without understanding the process and transmission mechanism that lower the effectiveness of standard policies, policy makers may be tempted to try bigger doses of the same monetary policy when intended results are not met. This will actually increase the risk of bankruptcies. Instead, the distinct characteristics of capital flows during the three phases of global liquidity point to the need for early warning indicators to evolve and be adjusted for each phase. Based on the analyses and the more relevant early warning indicators, we argue a set of macroprudential policies is needed to complement monetary policy.

Chapter 2
The Three Phases of Global Liquidity

The external environment is an important backdrop in determining economic policy. Economies with open financial systems and convertible capital accounts are sensitive to global market conditions. Even economies with less open financial systems are affected. Those with liberalized trade and partially controlled financial systems are also influenced—through current account transactions and their financial repercussions.

In this chapter, we describe three recent phases of global liquidity and discuss the policy implications of each for emerging Asia.[1] The first phase is the period leading up to the 2008/2009 global financial crisis (GFC) and the immediate aftermath of the September 2008 Lehman Brothers collapse. This phase is marked by an expansion in global banking and the transmission of financial conditions across borders through capital flows—intermediated by the global banking system. The concept of core and noncore liabilities is central, as they help define the level of risk-taking and the expansion of leverage and bank balance sheets.

The second phase of global liquidity begins roughly in 2010, when several central banks in advanced economies began using quantitative easing (QE) and asset purchase policies. These affected bond markets—both sovereign and corporate—and led to much easier conditions in the fixed-income securities market—such as higher durations, lower long-term yields, and increased volatility. In emerging Asia, the result was the rapid growth of local currency (LCY) bond markets. Real money asset managers—rather than banks—are the protagonists in this second phase of global liquidity. The search for yield led to an explosion in issuance from borrowers previously shunned by markets as being too risky or marginal. Credit

[1] Broadly, emerging Asia comprises Brunei Darussalam; Cambodia; the People's Republic of China (PRC); Hong Kong, China; Indonesia; India; the Republic of Korea; the Lao People's Democratic Republic (Lao PDR); Malaysia; Myanmar; the Philippines; Singapore; Taipei,China; Thailand; and Viet Nam. Due to limited data for some economies, figures in this chapter may use a subset of the group, but is still referred to as "Emerging Asia."

I.J. Azis and H.S. Shin, *Managing Elevated Risk*,
DOI 10.1007/978-981-287-284-5_2

expanded through corporate bond markets open to international investors, both in local currencies and in those of advanced economies, particularly the US dollar.

The May 2013 so-called taper tantrum—after the US Federal Reserve (US Fed) announced its intention to taper QE—and the financial squall that followed in emerging markets is our third phase of global liquidity. Large capital outflows from emerging Asia were linked to the impending end of easy money—as central banks in advanced economies said they would gradually "normalize" monetary policy. While emerging Asia remains much more capable of weathering external shocks than it was when the 1997/1998 Asian financial crisis struck, the "taper tantrum" turmoil exposed several vulnerabilities policy makers had not fully recognized. Capital flow reversals are certainly not new—they underscore the openness and interdependence of emerging Asian financial sector with global markets. Yet, without understanding the nature of capital flows in the first and second phases—particularly the growing size and role played by the region's capital markets—it is easy to ignore the limitations of standard policy measures. A certain policy may be less effective, while the risks it creates can be greater than when the region's capital markets were still in their infancy. Thus, a careful assessment of the benefits and costs of each policy is needed.

In the next section, we begin by examining the conceptual building blocks needed to understand the three phases of global liquidity. In particular, we review the accounting principles based on national income accounting and net capital flows that underpin the conventional approach to capital flows. This leads us to the gross capital flows—along with bank and corporate consolidated accounts—that expose otherwise hidden vulnerabilities. Afterward, we outline the three phases of global liquidity and provide an overview of empirical evidence especially as it pertains to Asia.

2.1 Conceptual and Measurement Issues

Measurement in international finance traditionally begins with national income accounting, with the aim of measuring aggregate output within a well-defined "economic territory," based on the residence principle. An economic entity (such as a firm, or more generally an "enterprise") is resident in an economic territory if its principal economic activity is conducted within its territorial boundaries. National income accounts further classify the activity into sectors and subsectors based on its output. The territorial boundary often coincides with national borders, but not always. The principle of measurement is based on residence rather than nationality. So even when headquartered elsewhere, a firm is counted as part of the aggregate activity of the territory if it conducts business within its boundaries.[2]

[2] BIS (2012) offers an introduction to the conceptual distinctions in measurement of international financial positions.

Boundaries serve two other roles in international finance given the convenience of defining aggregated data. First, the national income boundary is often used in aggregate economic models to define the decision-making unit. Thus, residents are aggregated into a representative individual that follows an aggregate consumption function. In particular, for example, the balance sheet of the decision-making unit is defined by the boundary set by national income accounting. The balance of payments and capital flows are defined by reference to increases in assets and liabilities of those inside the boundary against those outside. So capital inflows are defined as the increase in liabilities of residents to nonresidents, where the measurement is taken in net terms—they represent the increase in liabilities of residents to nonresidents net of any increase in claims of residents against nonresidents. As the measurement unit is the representative individual within the national income boundary, the restriction to net capital flows is quite natural.

Second, in simple economic models, the national income boundary also defines the currency area of a particular currency, so the real exchange rate between two national income territories is defined as the ratio of the prices between the two economic territories. The nominal exchange rate is defined as the price of one currency relative to another. Thus, implicitly, central bank monetary policy within the boundary affects residents within the boundary. To the extent monetary policy has spillover effects, either they may be captured through current account and trade balances, or they may be captured through capital inflows and outflows as measured in terms of residence.

To recap, the boundary of an "economic territory" in international economics serves three roles: (i) it is the boundary relevant for national income accounting; (ii) it defines the decision-making unit, especially its balance sheet; and (iii) it distinguishes domestic from foreign currency (FCY).

The three roles of the national income boundary is a convention followed in simplified economic models—even if the triple coincidence is not a logical consequence of output measurement. However, simple economic models that incorporate the triple coincidence were formulated and refined at a time when capital flows were not as central as they are today. Nonetheless, the simplification has served a useful purpose. Before financial globalization, the triple coincidence in the use of economic boundaries was a good approximation. However, with financial globalization, the triple coincidence has come increasingly under strain. Here, we recognize that the traditional role of national income boundary may not work as well in understanding today's global financial markets.

Before examining the impact of global market conditions on emerging Asia, it helps to see what happened in advanced economies in the run-up to the GFC and how European banks intermediated US dollar funding between savers and borrowers in the US.

Two separate periods of global liquidity should be examined. The first—phase one—roughly began in 2003 and lasted until the 2008/2009 GFC. Global banking was at its center. Loose financial conditions were transmitted across borders through accelerating capital flows using banks. In this context, global bank leverage explains comovements in financial conditions across geography and across sectors.

2.2 First Phase of Global Liquidity

The first phase of global liquidity shows the importance of drawing the correct accounting boundaries for measurement in international finance. In particular, the US subprime crisis highlights the importance of tracking gross capital flows. Borio and Disyatat (2011) have argued that the traditional net capital flow measure as given by the current account imbalance may be a potentially misleading measure of financial vulnerability. European banks role in intermediating US dollar funding was discussed by Shin (2012). Cetorelli and Goldberg (2008, 2010) provide extensive evidence using bank-level data to demonstrate that capital markets reallocate funding within global banking organizations.

2.2.1 Round-Trip Bank Flows to the US

During the first phase, European banks played a pivotal role in global financial flows. They effectively sustained the shadow banking system in the US by drawing on dollar funding in the wholesale market to lend to US residents through the purchase of securitized claims on US borrowers (Fig. 2.1).

Although their presence in the domestic US commercial banking sector was small, the shadow banking system made the impact of these European global banks on overall credit conditions much larger. This role underscores the importance of tracking gross capital flows.

European global banks intermediate US dollar funds in the US by drawing on wholesale dollar funding—for instance, from US money market funds (MMFs), which are then reinvested in securities ultimately backed by US mortgage assets. Capital first flows out of the US and then back in. This way, the cross-border flows

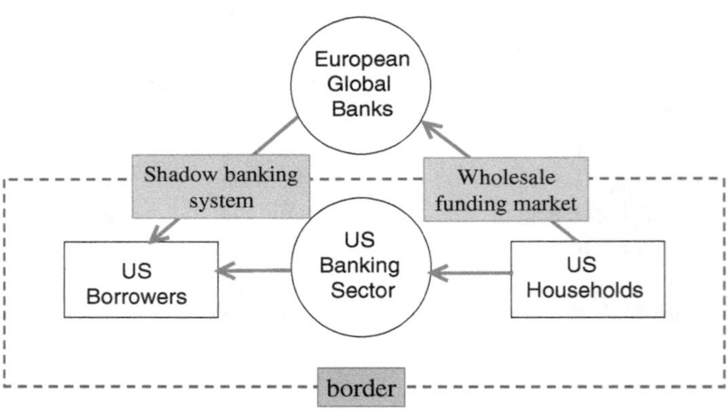

Fig. 2.1 European banks in the US shadow banking system. *Source* Shin (2012)

generated net out and thus do not appear as imbalances in the current account. Based on the Bank for International Settlements (BIS) banking statistics and information on borrowers from US MMF holdings, it is revealed that in the run-up to the GFC, MMFs in the US were the base of the shadow banking system, recycling wholesale funding to US borrowers via the balance sheet capacity of banks, especially European banks.

The amount owed by banks to US prime MMFs—based on the top 10 prime MMFs—represented $755 billion of the approximate $1.66 trillion total in prime MMF assets, classified by nationality of the borrowing bank (Fig. 2.2). US prime MMFs nearly bailed out completely from the European Union (EU) periphery as of the second half of 2011, as a snapshot of the dollar amounts by nationality of borrowing banks on 30 June 2011 makes clear (Fig. 2.3).

How gross flows net out is shown in Fig. 2.4, which plots US gross capital flows by category. Positive quantities (and bars) indicate gross capital inflows (the increase in claims of foreigners on the US), while negative quantities indicate gross capital outflows (the increase in claims of US residents on foreigners).

The gray-shaded bars indicate the increase in claims of official creditors on the US. This includes the increase in claims of the People's Republic of China (PRC) and other current account surplus economies. While official flows are large, private sector gross flows are larger still. The negative bars before 2008 indicate large outflows of capital from the US (principally through banks), which then re-enter the economy through purchases of non-Treasury securities.

We can gain additional insights on the nature of the gross capital flows through the banking system by following interbank claims of foreign banks operating in the US.

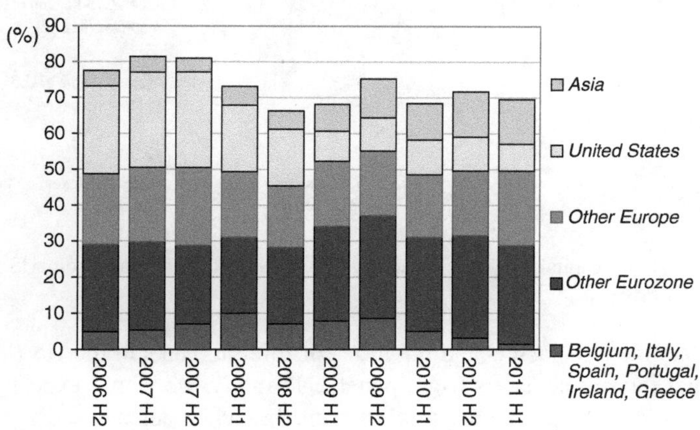

Fig. 2.2 Amount owed by banks to US prime money market funds (% of total, by nationality of borrowing bank). *Source* Fitch; and *Global Financial Stability Report October* 2011, International Monetary Fund

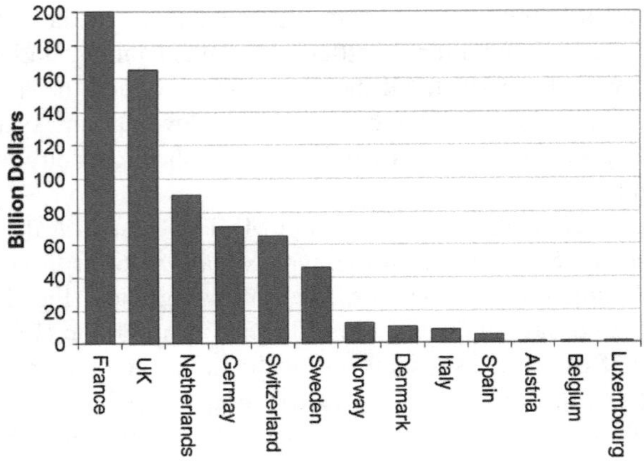

Fig. 2.3 Amount owed by banks to US prime money market funds (as of June 30, 2011, by nationality of borrowing bank). *Source* Fitch; and *Global Financial Stability Report October* 2011, International Monetary Fund

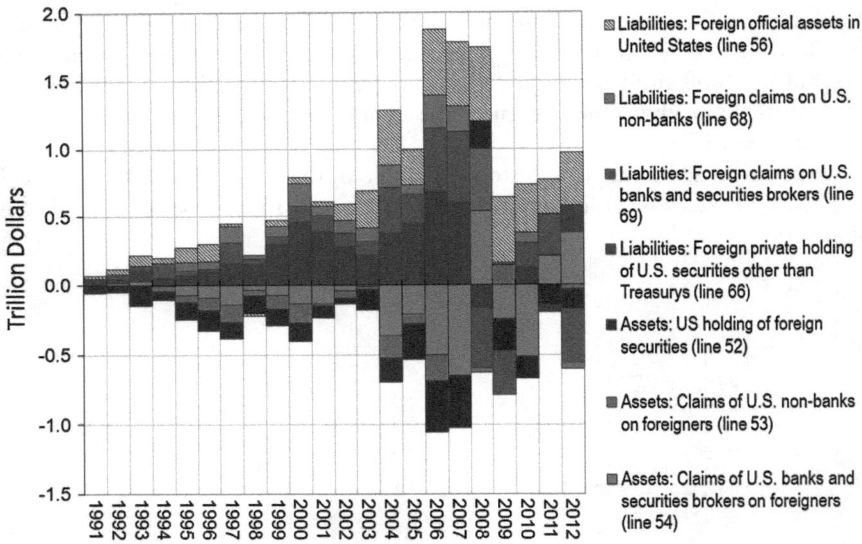

Fig. 2.4 US annual capital flows by category. *Source* Shin (2012); data from US Bureau of Economic Analysis

Figure 2.5 plots the assets and liabilities of foreign banks in the US (left panel) and their net interoffice assets (right panel). Normally, we would expect net interoffice assets to be negative, as foreign bank branches act as lending outposts. However, the decade between 2001 and 2011 was exceptional, when net interoffice assets turned sharply positive, before reversing into negative territory during 2011. Foreign bank branches and subsidiaries in the US are treated as US resident banks in the balance of payments, which are based on residence, not nationality.

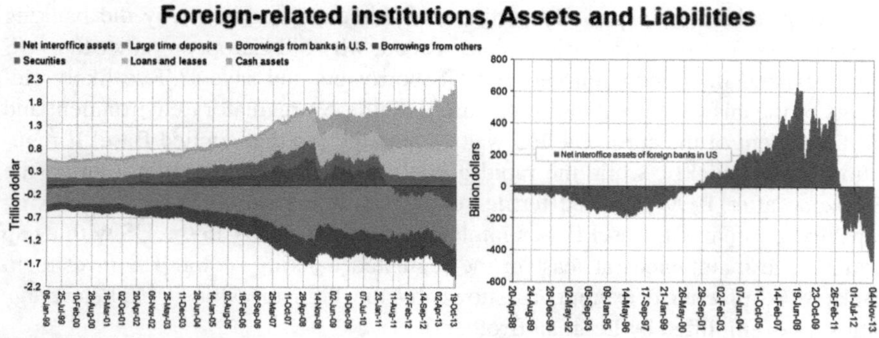

Fig. 2.5 Net interoffice assets of foreign banks in the US. *Source* H8 series on commercial banks, Federal Reserve Board

Therefore, Fig. 2.5 sheds light on the nature of gross capital outflows as shown in the balance of payments.

The schematic of the round-trip capital flows through European banks (see Fig. 2.1) is useful in understanding gross flows. European banks' US branches and subsidiaries drove the gross capital outflows through the banking sector by raising wholesale funding from US MMFs and then shipping them to headquarters.

Gross capital flows to the US through European bank lending via the shadow banking system played a pivotal role in influencing US credit conditions in the run-up to the subprime crisis. However, since the Eurozone had a roughly balanced current account—the UK was actually a deficit economy—their collective net capital flows vis-à-vis the US do not reflect the influence of their banks in setting overall US credit conditions.

The distinction between net and gross flows is a classic theme in international finance. But it deserves renewed attention given the new patterns of international capital flows. Focusing on the current account and the global savings glut obscures the role of gross capital flows and the "global banking glut."

The role of European banks shows the importance of drawing the right boundaries in international finance. Capital flows are traditionally viewed as the financial counterpart to savings and investment decisions, in line with the narrative of capital flowing "downhill" from capital-rich countries with lower rates of return to capital-poor countries with higher returns. From this perspective, the focus is typically on net capital flows, as that is what counts in funding an economy's borrowing requirements.

However, in the case of European banks intermediating US dollar funding, the boundary defined for national income accounting is crossed twice, so that the usual net flows do not capture the financial intermediaries engaging in the maturity transformation in the mortgage market. Of course, net capital flows are also of concern to policy makers. Current account imbalances have implications for the long-run sustainability of the net external asset position.

However, if the objective is to gauge credit conditions and overall financial vulnerability, the current account was of limited use in gauging overall credit conditions in the run-up to the 2008 GFC. Rather than the global savings glut, a more plausible culprit for subprime lending in the US was the global banking glut.

Two questions are especially pertinent in this context. First, why did banking capacity rise so rapidly in Europe? And second, why did European rather than US banks expand intermediation between US borrowers and savers? Two likely elements of the answer to both questions are (i) Europe's regulatory environment and (ii) the advent of the euro. The EU was the jurisdiction that applied Basel II regulations more quickly, while the rapid growth of cross-border banking within the Eurozone after 1999 provided fertile conditions for upscaling European banking capacity. By contrast, Basel II was implemented more slowly in the US with a cap on leverage maintained (at least in the regulated banking sector; US investment banks were of course exempt, as shown by the high investment bank leverage ratios, as exemplified by Lehman Brothers).

2.2.2 Banking Sector Flows to the Rest of the World

Figure 2.6 shows the cross-border banking sector claims of BIS-reporting banks against counterparties for a diverse group of economies. There is a high degree of synchronization of bank flows across the disparate geographies of recipient economies. At the same time, there is also a measure of diversity in the pattern of flows.

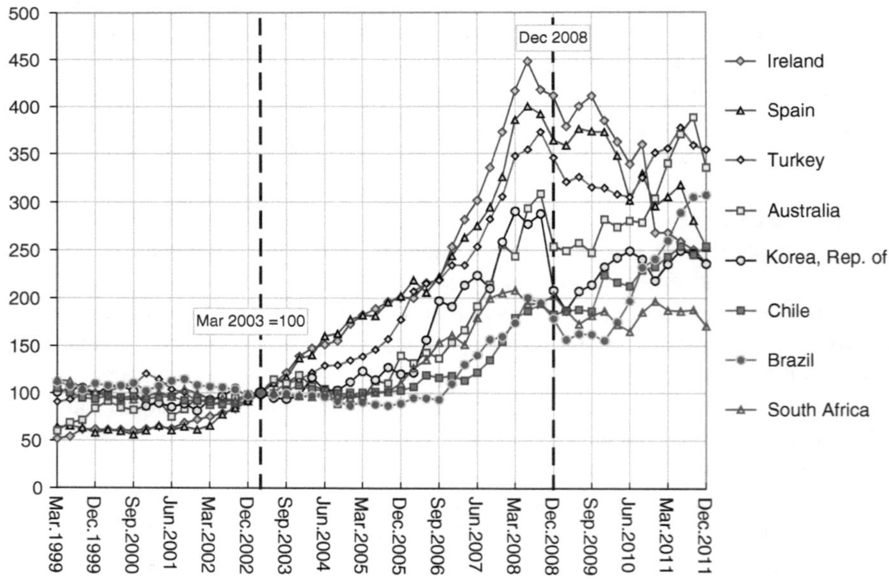

Fig. 2.6 Claims of BIS-reporting banks on counterparties in selected economies (March 2003 = 100). *Source* Bruno and Shin (2012); data from *Locational Banking Statistics*, Bank for International Settlements (BIS)

Emerging Europe saw the most rapid increase in banking sector inflows during the period, followed by countries such as the Republic of Korea and Turkey.

This suggests a global push factor that drove financial conditions globally, running through banks. It affected domestic financial conditions via the rapid expansion of bank lending funded by capital inflows.

Figure 2.7 depicts the institutional backdrop to the operation of the global banking system. Banks with access to the US dollar funding market through US MMFs channel funding from US financial markets to banks in other parts of the world (denoted as regions A, B, and C). The global banks include US-domiciled banks, but as discussed above, global banks with European headquarters were particularly active in channeling US dollar funding from the US to other parts of the world.

The interconnected nature of the global banking system generates spillover effects of financial conditions across borders. The greater ease in raising wholesale funding from the center through cheaper US dollar bank funding rates implies greater availability of funding to regional banks. This in turn translates into more lenient lending conditions to ultimate borrowers in regions A, B, C, etc. The global factors motivating the decisions of global banks will determine credit conditions in all locations through the institutional structure of the global banking system. The spillover effects thus generated mean that more accommodative credit conditions associated with global liquidity at the center lead to lower risk-adjusted lending rates, inducing firms to apply lower discount rates in their investment decisions. For any given fundamental cash flows, lower discount rates and higher net present values induce firms to take on more investment projects and greater risk.

Empirically, it has been shown that the leverage of the global banks at the center of the system can serve as a summary statistic for the activity of global banks in channeling funding from the center to the periphery. In this sense, global

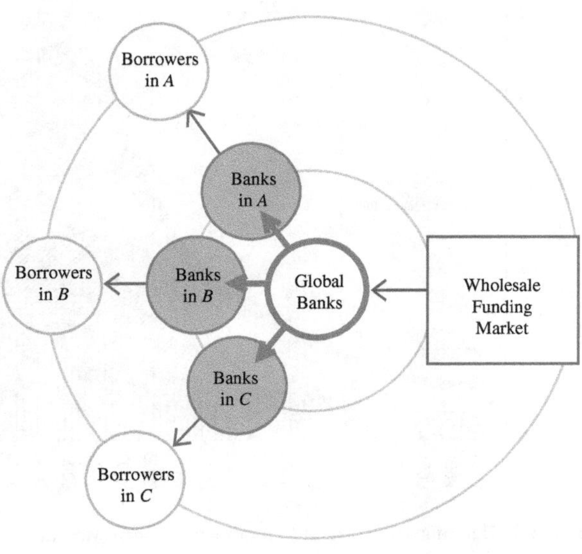

Fig. 2.7 Structure of the global banking system. *Source* Bruno and Shin (2013)

bank leverage turns out to be a useful proxy for the single global factor that determines credit availability to all borrowers across all peripheral economies.

Spain's experience is particularly instructive in how global liquidity converts capital flows into domestic credit growth. Total bank credit in Spain was EUR414 billion in December 1998, shortly before the economy joined the Eurozone. It subsequently increased fivefold to nearly EUR2 trillion in 2008 on the eve of the GFC (Fig. 2.8). At the time the euro was launched, domestic bank lending in Spain could be financed entirely from Spanish residents. But global liquidity changed all that, as capital flows and the lending boom fed off one another. At the peak of the cycle in 2008, only half of all bank lending in Spain was financed from domestic sources. The rest came from capital inflows as foreign banks had rapidly increased lending to Spanish banks (Fig. 2.9). This underscores how the Eurozone crisis is just part of a larger global picture. Global liquidity mirrors the procyclical nature of the global banking system.

Aside from being the world's most important reserve currency and invoicing currency for international trade, the US dollar also underpins the global banking system as the funding currency of choice for global banks. The US hosts branches of around 160 foreign banks, whose main function is to raise wholesale dollar funding in US capital markets and then ship the funds to their respective head offices.

Some of these borrowed dollars eventually find their way back to the US to finance purchases of mortgage-backed securities and other assets. But many of them flow to Europe, Asia, and Latin America where global banks are active local lenders. Thus, global banks become carriers for the transmission of cross-border liquidity spillovers. At the margin, the shadow value of bank funding is equalized

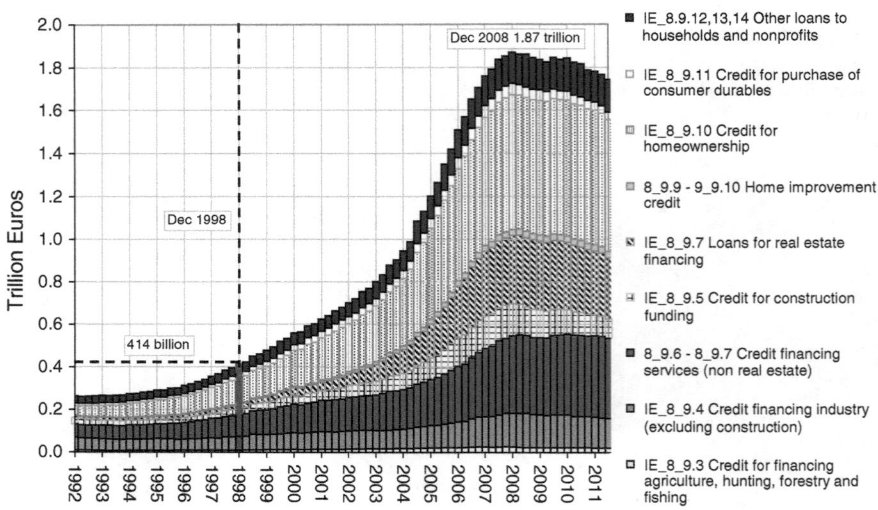

Fig. 2.8 Banking sector credit to nonfinancial borrowers in Spain. *Source* Bank of Spain

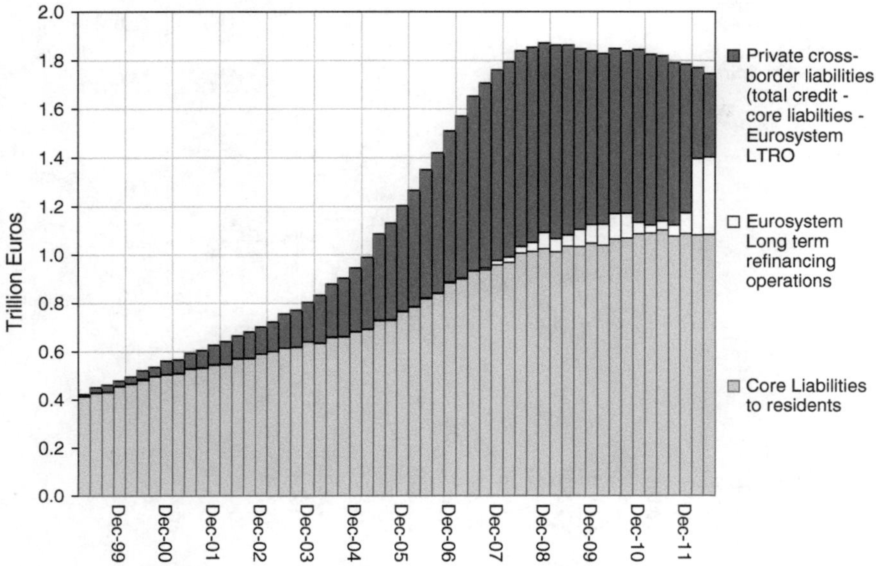

Fig. 2.9 Funding gap among Spanish Banks. *Source* Bank of Spain

across regions through portfolio decisions of global banks, so global banks become carriers of dollar liquidity across borders. In this way, permissive US liquidity condition is transmitted globally, and US monetary policy affects global financial conditions.

As noted earlier, the net interoffice assets of foreign banks in the US turned sharply positive before reversing during the height of the Eurozone crisis in 2011. During 2001–2011, foreign bank offices, rather than being lending outposts, in effect became funding sources for the parent bank. The net interoffice position of foreign banks in the US, therefore, reflects the extent to which global banks are engaged in supplying US dollar funding to other parts of the world. This is a reasonable proxy for the availability of wholesale funding provided to borrowers in a capital-recipient economy.

The large net positive interoffice accounts of foreign banks in the US highlight the potential for cross-border spillovers of monetary policy effects. Dollar funding shipped abroad to bank headquarters will be deployed globally based on portfolio allocation decisions that seek to maximize profitability. Thus, permissive liquidity conditions in the US dollar wholesale market will be transmitted via the global banking system to other parts of the world. Of course, the US dollar takes center stage as the currency underpinning the global banking system.

Figure 2.10 shows the FCY assets and liabilities of global banks as tracked by the BIS and arranged by currency. The US dollar series shows dollar assets and liabilities of banks outside the US, the euro series gives the EUR-denominated assets and liabilities of banks outside the Eurozone, and so on. The US dollar asset

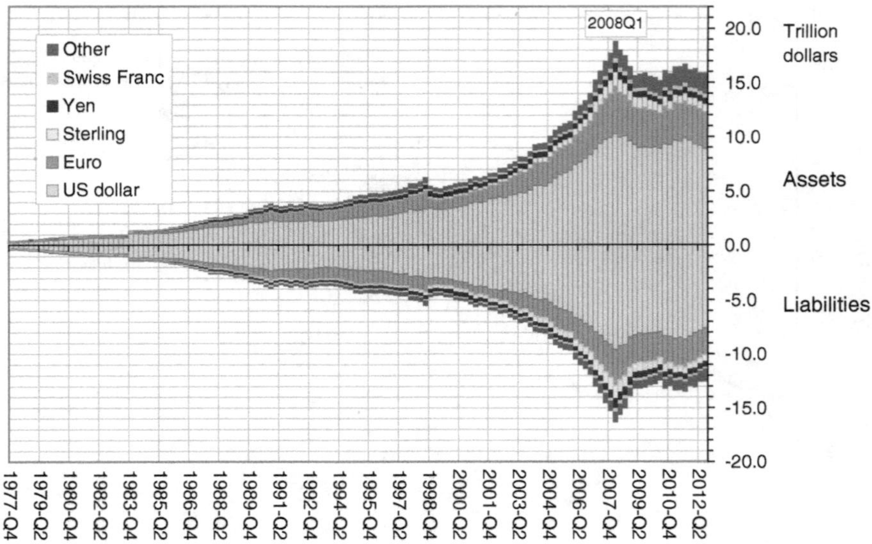

Fig. 2.10 Foreign currency assets and liabilities of BIS-reporting banks (by currency). *US* United States. *Source* BIS Locational Banking Statistics Table 5A, Bank for International Settlements (BIS)

series reached more than $10 trillion in 2008Q1, briefly exceeding the total assets of the US chartered commercial banking sector. Such a risk-taking channel is a powerful determinant of leverage, thereby acting as the linchpin in the propagation of global liquidity.

2.2.3 Exchange Rates and Leverage

Currency appreciation can fuel capital inflows rather than stem them, as currency appreciation strengthens local borrower balance sheets and creates additional slack in the lending capacity of banks, thereby stimulating further inflows. This is a distinctive feature of the risk-taking channel of capital flows through the banking system. This argument is developed in Bruno and Shin (2013), who construct a model of bank capital flows that track the balance sheet relationships in the global banking system, rather than follow the national income boundaries as in the conventional approach to capital flows.

The analysis highlights an important policy lesson. In dealing with capital inflows, a frequently encountered policy prescription is for the authorities of the capital-recipient economy to allow the currency to appreciate, engineering an expenditure switching effect from tradables to nontradables. However, when bank capital flows are involved, the prescription may not easily remedy the credit booms and manage capital inflow pressures. Indeed, policy makers are at risk of inadvertently creating an even bigger boom-bust episode.

To grasp this point, it is important to understand the link between currency appreciation and the buildup of overall bank leverage. The channel is through shifts in the effective credit risk faced by banks who lend to local borrowers that may hold a currency mismatch. When the LCY appreciates, local borrower balance sheets become stronger, resulting in lower credit risk and hence expanded bank lending capacity. In this way, currency appreciation leads to greater risk-taking by banks. This "risk-taking channel" of currency appreciation links exchange rates and financial stability.

Consider the example of a foreign bank branch lending in dollars to local borrowers who convert the proceeds of the dollar loan into LCY—possibly to hedge the currency risk from long-term export receivables, or to engage in outright speculation that the LCY will appreciate further. In this situation, an initial appreciation of the recipient economy's currency will strengthen the balance sheets of domestic borrowers who borrowed in dollars. As borrowers become more creditworthy, bank loan books show less risk, creating additional lending capacity. In this way, the initial impulse from an appreciating domestic currency can be amplified. A reinforcing mechanism exists through which greater bank risk-taking reduces credit risk, which drives even greater bank risk-taking and further appreciation of the domestic currency, thereby completing the circle.

In this setting, an appreciating domestic currency may not have the presumed effect of curtailing capital inflows. The upward phase of the cycle will give the appearance of a virtuous circle, in which the mutually reinforcing effect of real appreciation and improved balance sheets operate in tandem. Once the cycle turns, however, the amplification mechanism operates in reverse, reinforcing the financial distress of borrowers and the banking sector in general.

The rapid growth of a banking sector fueled by capital inflows and an appreciating currency has been a classic early warning indicator of emerging economy crises. Gourinchas and Obstfeld (2012) conduct an empirical study using data from 1973 to 2010 and find that two factors emerge consistently as the most robust and significant predictors of financial crises—a rapid increase in leverage and sharp real currency appreciation. This holds for both emerging and advanced economies and holds throughout the sample period. Schularick and Taylor (2012) similarly highlight the role of leverage in financial vulnerability, especially the leverage associated with the banking sector.

Economists have traditionally seen exchange rate appreciation driven by capital inflows as self-correcting. Once the currency has appreciated sufficiently, investors responsible for the capital inflows will recognize the change in the risk–return configuration and will therefore slow their investment. Indeed, the standard prescription of the official sector continues to follow a lexicographic ordering in which the real exchange rate should be allowed to appreciate sufficiently, and all the domestic macroeconomic policy responses should be exhausted before (and as a last resort) deploying measures to stem capital inflows directly.

Standard caveats of course accompany the standard prescription. Domestic distortions could be responsible for both capital inflows and exchange rate appreciation. For example, foreign investors may be willing to take long positions in the domestic economy, in particular in the short run, due to very high domestic interest rates. In this case, there may be a positive correlation between short-term inflows and exchange rate appreciation. But the ultimate cause will be a third factor—the distortion in domestic yields. Problems are exacerbated if monetary authorities then attempt to limit appreciation. Anticipated appreciation plus the high domestic interest rate will attract additional inflows, dooming any attempt to limit appreciation. The implication is that that policy makers should not attempt to use capital controls to defend policy inconsistencies, which many times cannot be resolved in the short run.[3]

When bank credit constitutes the bulk of inflows, there is an additional caveat to the standard prescription of letting the currency appreciate. The behavior of banks and other leveraged institutions is influenced by their capital position and perceived risks. Currency appreciation and strong profitability, coupled with tranquil economic conditions, can be seen by banks as a cue to further expand lending, leading to further capital inflows.

Therefore, the basic philosophical divide is between those who do and do not believe that real appreciation eventually chokes off capital inflows due to a reassessment of the attractiveness of the destination currency. Members of the first camp (the traditional view) believe that capital flows are driven by textbook portfolio investors who are driven by fundamental assessments of currency values, while members of the second camp believe that capital flows are driven not only by assessments of fundamental value but also by the short-term imperatives of bank balance sheet capacity—and what Borio and Disyatat (2011) refer to as the "excess elasticity" of credit.

For these reasons, macroprudential policy and monetary policy complement one another well when global liquidity is operating strongly, as prudential rules create sufficient space for domestic monetary policy to operate without the distortionary effects of capital flows.

2.3 Second Phase of Global Liquidity

The second phase of global liquidity appears through sovereign and corporate debt markets. Figure 2.11 plots trends in the outstanding amounts of international securities issued by governments in developing economies by region as defined by the BIS. The total outstanding amounts of international securities in each region are normalized to equal unity at the end of 2005Q1. Issuance from governments in Africa and the Middle East has grown rapidly since 2008, with amounts

[3] Chile's experience in the 1990s and Brazil's more recently highlight this point.

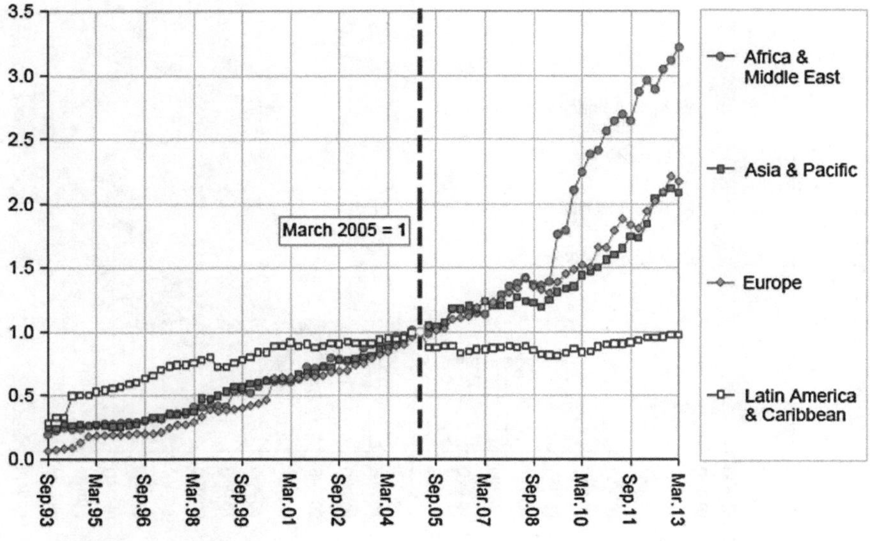

Fig. 2.11 Government international debt securities outstanding (2005Q1 = 1). *Source* Debt Securities Statistics, Bank for International Settlements

outstanding more than tripling since 2005Q1. Developing Asia and the Pacific and developing Europe also saw rapid increases, although less rapid than Africa. Developing Latin America, by contrast, did not see an increase in the amount of bonds outstanding.

This provides the contextual backdrop for the numerous international bond issues by "frontier" sovereigns in Africa and elsewhere who have only recently ventured into the international bond market.

The rapid pace of new issuance is perhaps even starker for nonfinancial corporate issuers in developing economies (Fig. 2.12). Corporate borrowers in emerging economies have increased their total international securities borrowing from less than \$200 billion in the aftermath of the Lehman crisis to \$450 billion by March 2013. Here, corporate borrowers in Latin America have increased borrowing sharply, in contrast to the subdued borrowing activity of Latin American sovereigns.

During the "taper tantrum" of May 2013, one conceptual challenge was to reconcile what appeared to be the small net external debt position of many emerging economies with the apparently disproportionate impact of the promise of eventual tighter global monetary conditions on their currencies and financial markets.

One piece in the puzzle may be the role played by nonfinancial corporates (NFCs) that operate across borders. When corporate activity is conducted in more than one territory—as defined by the traditional national income border—measuring exposures at the national income border itself may not capture the strain on corporate balance sheets.

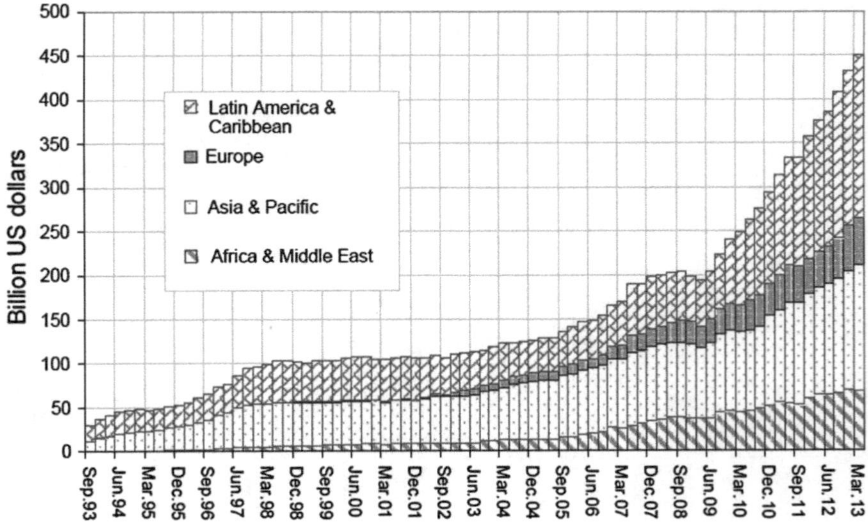

Fig. 2.12 Nonfinancial corporate international debt securities outstanding by developing region. *US* United States. *Source* **Debt Securities Statistics**, Bank for International Settlements

A schematic illustration of a multinational corporation borrowing US dollars through an overseas subsidiary—either from a global bank or from the corporate bond market—helps tell the tale (Fig. 2.13). If the proceeds of the borrowing are sent to headquarters through a capital account transaction, the traditional balance of payments accounts would show a net capital inflow in the form of greater external liabilities of the headquarters to its overseas subsidiary. However, if the multinational firm chooses to classify the transaction as part of trade flows in goods and

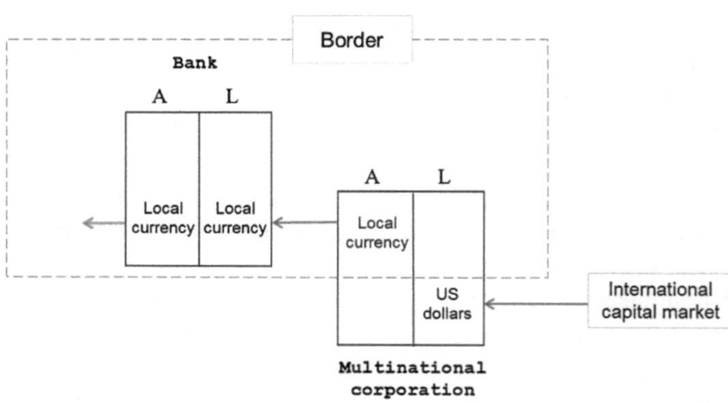

Fig. 2.13 Nonbank Firm as surrogate intermediary. *US* United States, *A* assets, *L* liabilities. *Source* Authors' illustration

services, the vulnerability of the multinational firm to external financial shocks may not be captured through the usual residence-based balance of payments accounts.

Drawing on the discussion in Azis and Shin (2013) helps illustrate the second phase of global liquidity and the importance of emerging market debt securities as the channel for emerging market borrowers to gain access to global capital markets.

There has been a clear shift from banks to the bond market since 2010 (Fig. 2.14). The black and white bars refer to borrowing by emerging market banks. The dark gray bars refer to borrowing by nonbanks. The numbers are net financing amounts for each year and hence denote increases in amounts outstanding. The white bars shrink rapidly, indicating that capital flows from global banks to emerging market banks have slowed to a trickle. Instead, emerging market banks have increased issuance in debt securities. For nonbanks, growth in net issuance of international debt securities has been even more dramatic.

The international debt securities numbers are based on a borrower's nationality rather than the usual practice of classifying them by residence (the reason "external" is in inverted commas). A borrower's nationality is defined by the location of its headquarters. If an emerging market corporate borrower issues corporate bonds through its overseas subsidiary—say in London—the usual balance of payments definition (based on residence) would treat the bonds as the liability of the UK entity. However, the emerging market company will manage its finances by reference to its consolidated balance sheet. Thus, it would be important to consider the consolidated balance sheet in explaining the behavior of the emerging market company, taking account of debt securities issued offshore to reconstruct the total assets and liabilities of the decision-making unit.

Offshore debt issuance by emerging market firms has expanded rapidly (McCauley et al. 2013). Figure 2.15 plots the international debt securities outstanding of borrowers from Brazil and the PRC, plotted by residence and

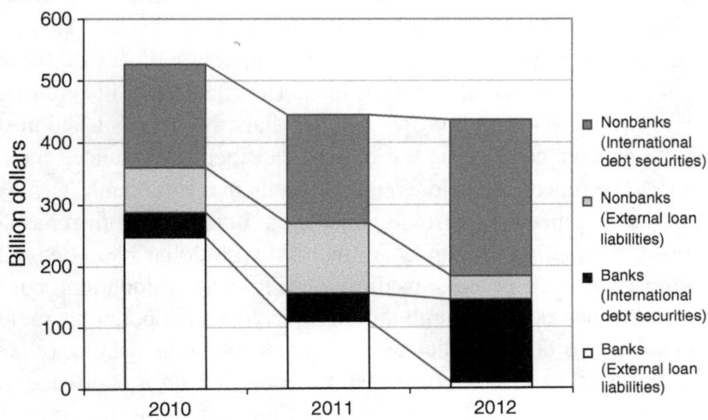

Fig. 2.14 Net "external" financing of emerging economies. *Source* Turner (2014)

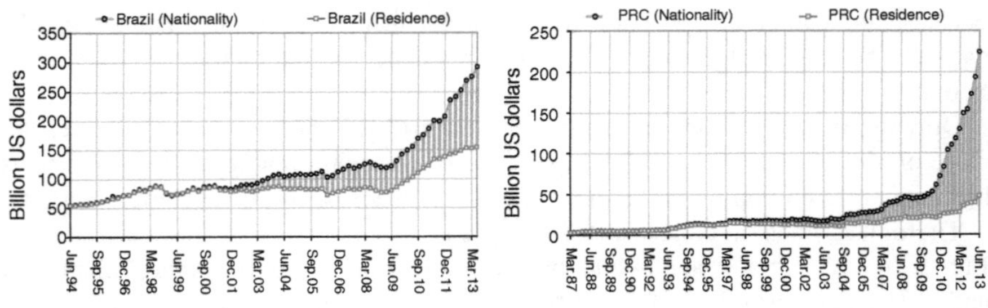

Fig. 2.15 International debt securities outstanding (all borrowers, by residence and nationality of issuer). *Source* BIS securities statistics Table 11A and 12A, Bank for International Settlements (BIS)

nationality. The difference between the two series reflects the offshore international debt securities issuance. It was small until after the GFC, but widened dramatically thereafter. The scale of the charts shows just how large the outstanding amounts are. Most offshore issuance has been in US dollars, so these corporates have become much more sensitive to US interest rates and exchange rates fluctuations.

This sheds light on what had been a puzzle. As mentioned earlier, the May 2013 "taper tantrum" and emerging market squall in January 2014 posed the quandary of reconciling small net external debt positions of many emerging economies (measured in usual residence terms) with the apparently disproportionate impact of the intention and then start of tighter global monetary conditions on their currencies and financial markets. One piece in the puzzle may be the role of offshore debt issuance by firms operating across borders. When corporate activity straddles borders, measuring exposures at the border itself may not capture the strain on corporate balance sheets.

There are two instances where a firm's true external exposure may not be captured in residence-based statistics (Fig. 2.16). The left panel shows a PRC corporate with an office in Hong Kong, China, borrowing US dollars from a Hong Kong, China bank, depositing renminbi in the bank's PRC office as collateral. This transaction resembles the London Eurodollar currency swap transaction of the 1960s and 1970s, which worked like a straight collateralized loan. The right panel illustrates schematically an Indian company which borrows in US dollars through its London subsidiary and defrays the group's costs using the dollars, but then accumulates Indian rupees at headquarters. The rupees are held as time deposits in a local bank in India. In both cases, the firm has engineered a currency mismatch. In effect, the firm has taken on a carry trade position, holding cash in LCY financed with dollar liabilities. Intra-group accounts would keep track of the subsidiary's claims on headquarters, but the accumulation of claims may occur through the firm's day-to-day operations rather than an explicit financial transaction classified as capital inflows on the balance of payments.

Thus, the standard external debt measures compiled on a residence basis may not fully reflect the true vulnerabilities relevant for explaining market behavior. If the overseas subsidiary of an emerging market company takes on US dollar debt

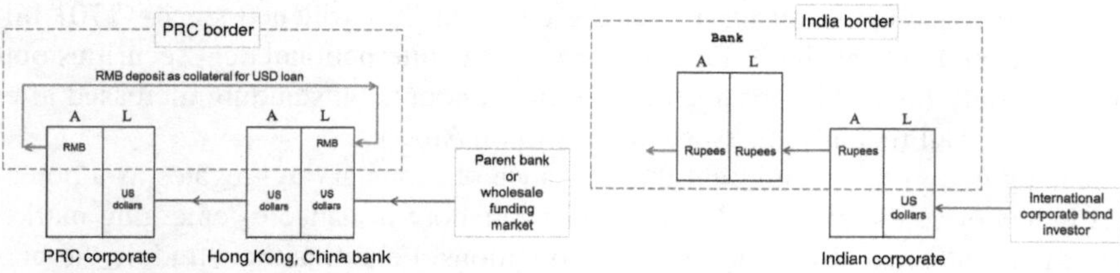

Fig. 2.16 Straddling the border through international transactions. *A* assets, *L* liabilities. *Source* Authors' illustration

holding LCY-denominated financial assets at headquarters, then the company as a whole faces a currency mismatch, even if no currency mismatch is captured in official net external debt statistics.

Nevertheless, the firm's fortunes (and hence actions) will be sensitive to currency movements and thus foreign exchange risk. One motive for taking the carry trade position may be to hedge export receivables. Alternatively, the carry trade position may be motivated by the prospect of financial gain should the domestic currency strengthen against the US dollar. In practice, however, the distinction between hedging and speculation may be difficult to draw.

Figure 2.17 plots the total international debt securities outstanding of all borrowers from developing economies as defined by the BIS, plotted by residence and by nationality. As before, the difference between the nationality and residence series accounts for the offshore issuance of international debt securities. Again, the

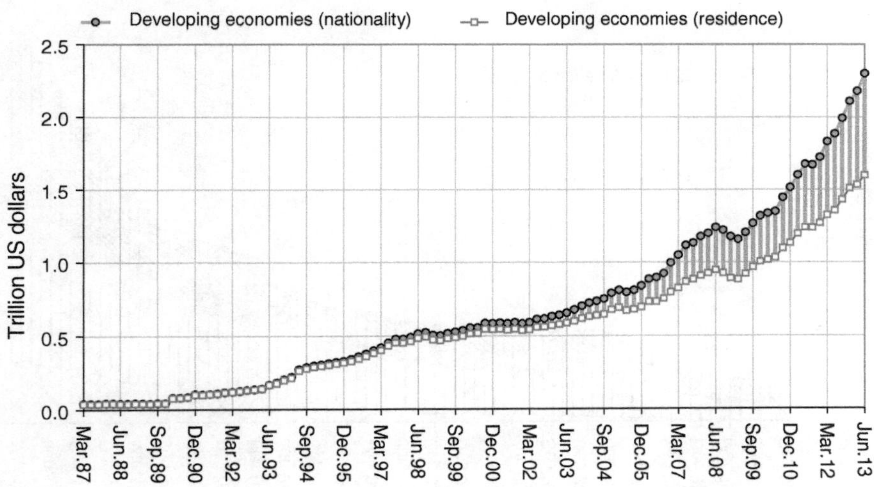

Fig. 2.17 International debt securities outstanding—developing economies (all borrowers, by nationality and residence of borrower). *Source* BIS securities statistics Table 11A and 12A, Bank for International Settlements (BIS)

difference remained small until after the GFC, but has widened since—$701 billion at the end of June 2013. Figure 2.18 plots the international debt securities outstanding only for NFCs, arranged by region. Amounts outstanding increased after the crisis for all regions, but especially for Latin America.

Chung et al. (2013) highlight the relevance of monetary aggregates as a potential indicator of the channel through which offshore issuance of emerging market firms may influence domestic financial conditions. For firms that straddle the border, their financial activities are likely to leave an imprint on the domestic financial system hosting its headquarters. If the firm issues debt offshore in FCY but accumulates liquid financial assets in domestic currency—in the form of claims on domestic banks or in the shadow banking system in the headquarter economy—then keeping track of the firm's corporate deposits and short-term financial assets will give an indirect indication of its overseas financial activities and hence the broad financial conditions that prevail in international capital markets. Chung et al. (2013) show that external financial conditions are reflected in the monetary aggregates of capital-recipient economies through the increased size of corporate deposits, as measured by the IMF's International Financial Statistics (IFS). As the firm will borrow more under permissive financial conditions, we would expect to see the conjunction of both the firm's increased indebtedness and greater holdings of cash and short-term investments on the consolidated balance sheet. In other words, the firm's financial assets and financial liabilities will increase together, as verified in Shin and Zhao (2013). This way, the greater NFC claims on the domestic banking system may reflect the indirect impact of more permissive financial conditions

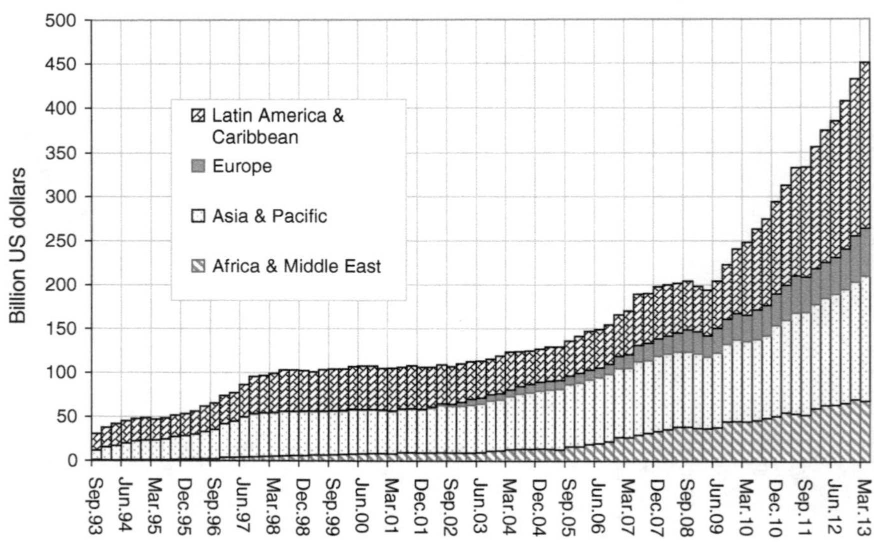

Fig. 2.18 Nonfinancial corporates' international debt securities outstanding—developing economies (by nationality of issuer). *Source* BIS Debt Securities Statistics, Bank for International Settlements (BIS)

globally. Also, to the extent there is a global factor driving global financial conditions, we would expect NFC claims globally to fluctuate in line with global financial conditions. So measures on the liability side of a bank's balance sheet may be a superior indicator of overall credit conditions than tracking the asset side as a whole. The advantage of liability measures comes from the role NFCs play "straddling" the border. Their activities are not easily monitored through usual external debt measures using locational definitions in balance of payments and national income statistics.

2.4 The Case of Emerging Asia

The first and second phases of global liquidity have important implications for emerging Asia. For our analysis, we break down capital flows into four types: "foreign direct investment" (FDI); "equities" (equity portfolios); "debt" (debt securities and other debt including derivatives); and "bank" (capital flows intermediated by the banking sector). Bank-led and debt-led flows are the most volatile among the four types.

Debt-led and bank-led capital flows shifted from negative to positive in five Asian economies during the second half of the 2000s (Fig. 2.19).[4]

Classifying capital flow trends into "surges" (a sharp increase in inflows), "stops" (a sharp decrease in inflows), "flight" (a sharp increase in outflows), and "retrenchment" (a sharp decrease in outflows), the following pattern emerges for the economies cited above:

- Surges: equity-led in 2009Q4–2010Q1; debt-led in 2002Q2, 2005Q4, and 2007Q2–2007Q4; bank-led in 2004Q1 and 2010Q2
- Stops: equity-led in 2008Q1–2008Q3; debt-led in 1997Q1–1997Q3 and 1998Q3; and bank-led in 1997Q4–1998Q2 and 2008Q4–2009Q2
- Flight: equity-led in 2007Q4; debt-led in 2005Q4; bank-led in 1999Q3, 2001Q2, 2002Q4–2004Q3, 2006Q1–2006Q2, 2007Q2–2007Q3, and 2010Q1
- Retrenchment: debt-led in 1997Q3–1998Q2 and 2008Q2; bank-led in 1996Q4–1997Q1, 1998Q3–1998Q4, 2002Q1, 2005Q2, and 2008Q3–2009Q2

For South Asia, the following pattern was observed:

- Surges: equity-led in 2003Q4, 2007Q2–2007Q4, and 2010Q1; debt-led in 2004Q4–2005Q3 and 2006Q4–2007Q1; bank-led in 2003Q2–2003Q3, 2004Q1, and 2008Q1
- Stops: equity-led in 1998Q2 and 2008Q3–2009Q1; debt-led in 2000Q1, 2002Q1–2002Q2, and 2009Q2

[4] Indonesia, Japan, the Republic of Korea, the Philippines, and Thailand. While Japan is not considered an emerging Asian economy, we include it here for a bigger data set.

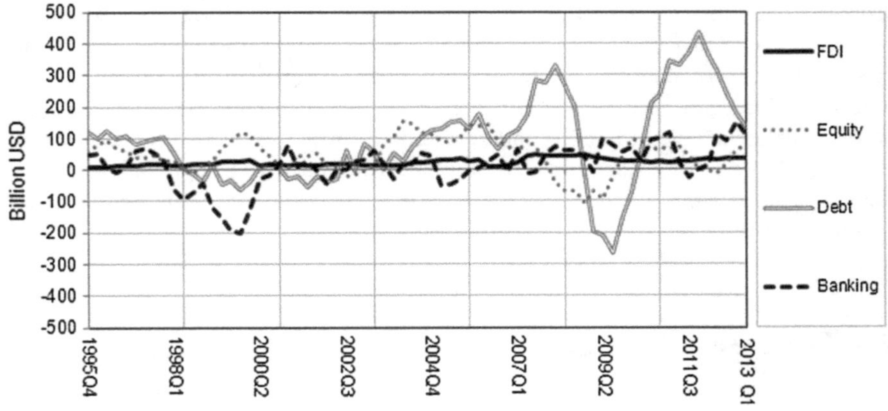

Fig. 2.19 Gross capital inflows—selected East Asian economies. *FDI* foreign direct investment. *Note* Data include gross capital inflows for Indonesia, Japan, the Republic of Korea, the Philippines, and Thailand. *Source* ADB calculations using data from International Monetary Fund Balance of Payments Statistics

- Flight: equity-led in 2006Q1, 2006Q4–2007Q2, and 2012Q3–2012Q4; debt-led in 2000Q4–2001Q2, 2004Q2, and 2008Q4; bank-led in 2004Q1 and 2009Q1
- Retrenchment: equity-led in 2011Q2–2011Q4; debt-led in 2000Q1, 2001Q4–2002Q2, and 2007Q3; bank-led in 1998Q4–1999Q4, 2002Q3, and 2007Q4–2008Q2

For bank-led flows, deleveraging by European banks contributed to the volatility. As funding conditions in Europe deteriorated toward the end of 2011, bleak economic prospects and doubts over fiscal sustainability undermined the value of sovereign and other assets. Bond issuance by banks fell, especially uncollateralized issuance in economies with fiscal problems; outflows due to fund withdrawals surged, particularly in Italy and Spain, and exposure to several EU financial institutions dropped sharply.

Capital flows to Asia intensified before the GFC (Figs. 2.20 and 2.21). These flows can be beneficial, but their volatile pattern and procyclicality can also act as a channel that transmits the buildup of financial risks and imbalances. A recent study examining the procyclicality of financial systems in Asia confirms that bank liabilities are highly procyclical, as indicated by the significantly positive real gross domestic product (GDP) elasticities, although the degree of procyclicality varies across economies. In economies with relatively high real GDP elasticities, such as the Republic of Korea and Indonesia, noncore liabilities are more procyclical than core liabilities. Also, noncore liabilities such as foreign borrowings tend to be more procyclical during boom periods. Using a slightly different approach, in Chap. 4, we also find evidence of procyclicality in selected Asian economies.

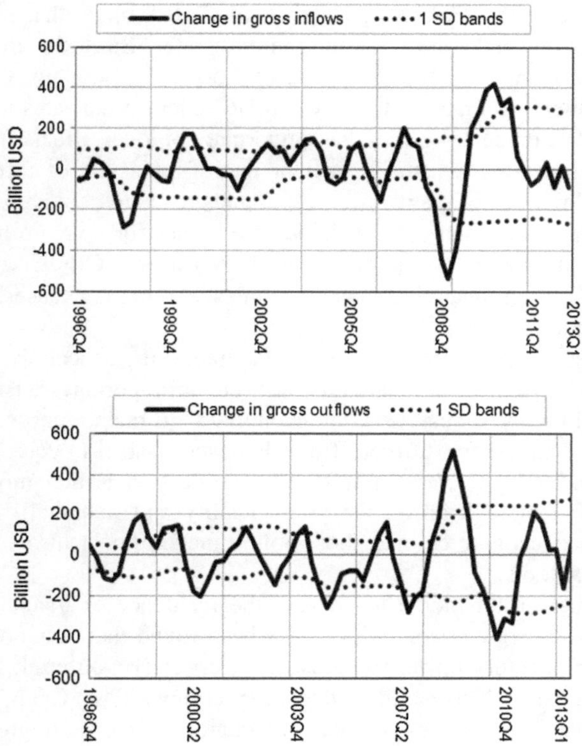

Fig. 2.20 Gross capital inflows and outflows—selected Asian economies. *SD* standard deviation. *Notes* Data include gross capital inflows and outflows for Indonesia, Japan, the Republic of Korea, the Philippines, and Thailand, computed as year-on-year change based on a 4-quarter moving sum. Inflows refer to bank flows from other investments on the liabilities side (assigned a positive value); outflows refer to bank flows from other investments on the assets side (assigned a negative value). *Source* ADB calculations using data from the International Monetary Fund Balance of Payments Statistics

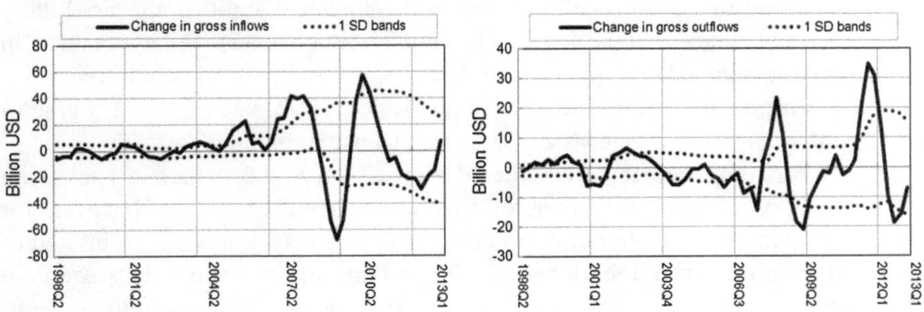

Fig. 2.21 Gross capital inflows and outflows in selected South Asian economies. *SD* standard deviation. *Notes* Data for South Asia include India, Pakistan, and Sri Lanka; periods covered = 1995Q1–2013Q1 for India and Pakistan and 1995Q1–2011Q4 for Sri Lanka, computed as year-on-year change based on a 4-quarter moving sum; inflows refer to bank flows from other investments on the liabilities side (assigned a positive value); outflows refer to bank flows from other investments on the assets side (assigned a negative value). *Source* ADB calculations using data from the International Monetary Fund Balance of Payments Statistics

Regarding US monetary policy, Hahm et al. (2013) show that bank liabilities respond to both domestic and US policy interest rates. But there are some differences across economies. In the Republic of Korea and Singapore, for example, bank liabilities tend to increase faster when US federal fund rates are low, which indicates that US monetary policy has important spillover effects on bank leveraging in emerging Asia. On the impact of interoffice assets of foreign banks in the US, bank liabilities in many Asian economies respond positively to US cross-border interoffice loans and the elasticities are higher for noncore liabilities. The impact of global market uncertainty, as measured by the CBOE Volatility Index (VIX), seems less significant in Asian economies, and in many cases, the elasticity has an opposite sign.

Overall, these suggest that noncore bank liabilities, especially foreign bank borrowings, are highly procyclical and constitute an important transmission channel of global liquidity shocks to Asian economies. In open emerging economies, financial cycles can be far different from domestic business cycles due to cross-border links through noncore funding. The implication is that monetary policy alone is insufficient to lean against procyclicality and financial cycles in open emerging market economies, and thus, policy makers must also have access to macroprudential tools.

Using a panel probit model to analyze the incidence of financial crises in a large sample of emerging economies, it has been found that noncore bank liabilities do have explanatory power for subsequent crises (Hahm et al. 2011). This is consistent with the analysis based on data of emerging Asia in Chap. 4. The empirical performance of measures for noncore liabilities is encouraging even when more traditional measures are included, such as the ratio of credit to GDP. In particular, banks' foreign liabilities are a major component of their noncore liabilities in many emerging market economies where the domestic wholesale bank funding market is not yet able to support rapid bank lending growth.

The overall results from these studies are consistent with the hypothesis that noncore bank liabilities matter more in open emerging market economies than in relatively closed ones. However, the impact of noncore liabilities appears highly nonlinear and heterogeneous across different crisis episodes. Policy makers in emerging Asia must take these complex interactions and their effects into consideration when pursuing capital market liberalization. They need to craft a careful macroprudential policy framework as a guard against potential risks.

For an economy like the Republic of Korea, where the domestic banks can access the global banking system for funding, this makes sense. However, for financial systems at an earlier development stage, or where banks are prohibited or restricted from accessing the global banking system, the distinction between core and noncore liabilities will look different, although the principles from the system-wide accounting framework will continue to apply (discussed in more detail in Chap. 3).

Regardless of system openness, however, a large increase of highly volatile debt-led and bank-led flows pose a difficult challenge for policy makers in maintaining macro- and financial stability. Bank-led flows can alter the size and composition of bank balance sheets to the point that risk of a banking crisis increases. On the asset side, loan-to-value ratios can rise quickly due to excessive credit expansion and other forms of risky investment, while an increase in noncore liabilities through bank-led flows can heighten risky behavior and increase bank leverage. Bank credit can also be disrupted when an external shock strikes. With a stronger currency resulting from capital inflows, banks are willing to take greater risks by extending more credit as the balance sheet of borrowers improves.

These risks are particularly important for bank-dependent Asian economies with open capital accounts—where bank leverage tends to exceed cyclical norms. Bank credit growth in emerging Asia accelerated prior to the GFC (Fig. 2.22). Even afterward, growth continued to rise in some economies. This rapid expansion coincided with rising demand for real estate, causing a persistent increase in property prices and exposing the region to the risk of a bubble bursting. Credit for consumption also surged, which allowed relatively high economic growth amid the global economic slowdown.

We investigate the implications for bank behavior by using flow-of-funds (*FOF*) data from five Asian economies—Indonesia; the Republic of Korea; the Philippines; Taipei,China; and Thailand. The period under review is divided into pre-GFC (2000–2006) and GFC (2007–2011). In the set of charts in Fig. 2.23, the two periods are depicted as squares and triangles, respectively. We match the flow of different components of liabilities and assets based on the FOF data and estimate the trend line in both periods for each economy. In particular, we compare the (i) correlation of liabilities with total assets across different types of liabilities and (ii) the correlation of assets with noncore liabilities (or core liabilities in the case of households) across different types of assets (Azis and Yarcia 2014). The first aims to capture what type of liabilities moves in sync with changes in assets (source of funds); the second aims to identify the type of assets noncore liabilities invest in (use of funds).

For example, the Philippine financial sector exhibited a significant change in investment behavior between pre-GFC and GFC periods. The preference for noncore sources (nondeposits) increased, with the slope doubling, while the slope of currency and deposits declined. With growing noncore liabilities, financial sector investment is more diversified in favor of nonloans, particularly securities and equities. In the case of Indonesia, banks have been increasingly seeking funds from noncurrency and deposit sources. They continue to allocate the bulk of their funds for loans, presumably dominated by credit for consumption, real estate, and other nontradables. However, in both economies, the preference for securities and nonloan assets rose faster than that for lending.

Like Indonesia, the tendency in Thailand has been to allocate additional funds to loans. The corresponding loan slope is close to unity (0.99 and 0.93 during the pre-GFC and GFC periods, respectively). In the case of the Republic of Korea, the FOF data show a persistently strong tendency toward extending loans. Such a strong preference is depicted by a higher slope for loans than for nonloans. A shift of preference in favor of raising funds from noncore sources is also observed. The noncore share of banks' liabilities remained high, although it has been declining in recent years.

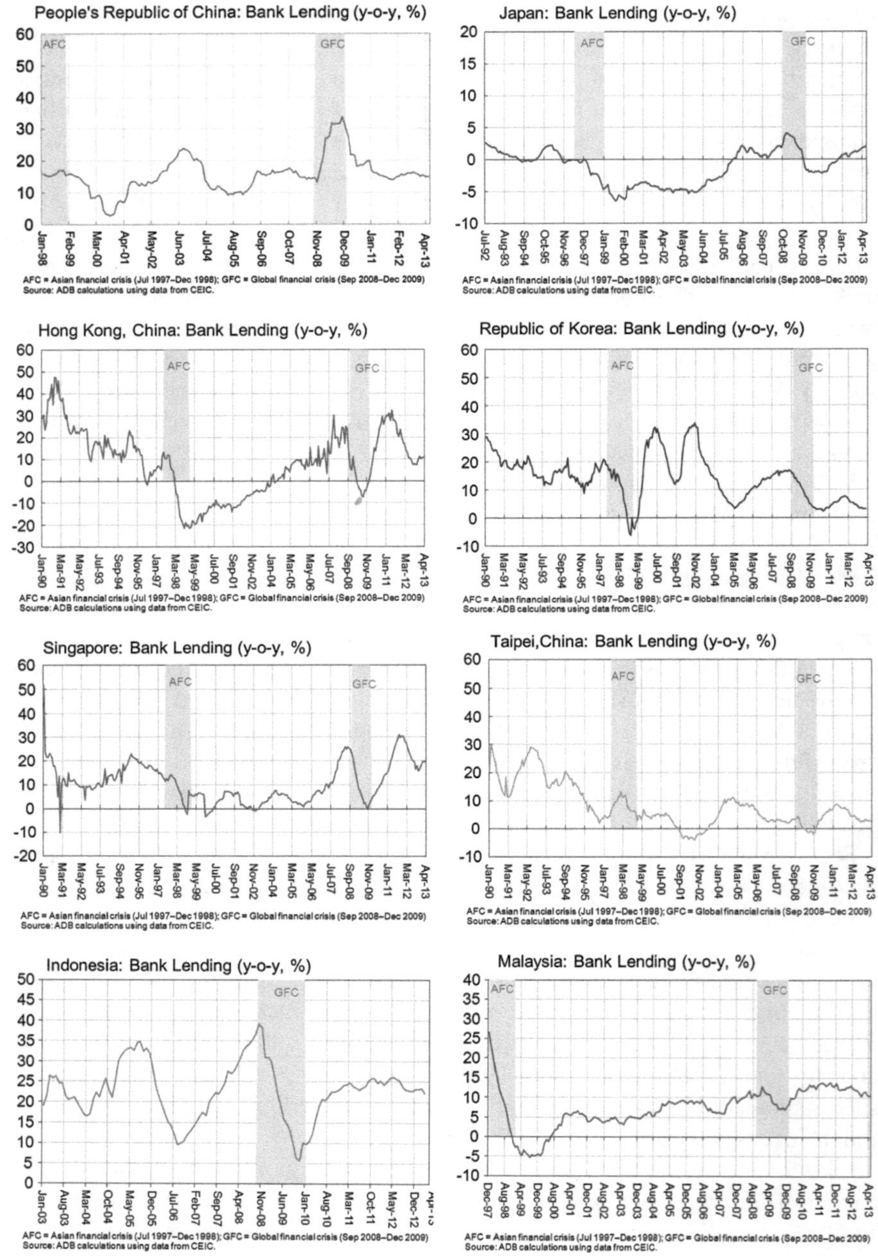

Fig. 2.22 Credit growth—emerging Asia. *Note y-o-y* year on year

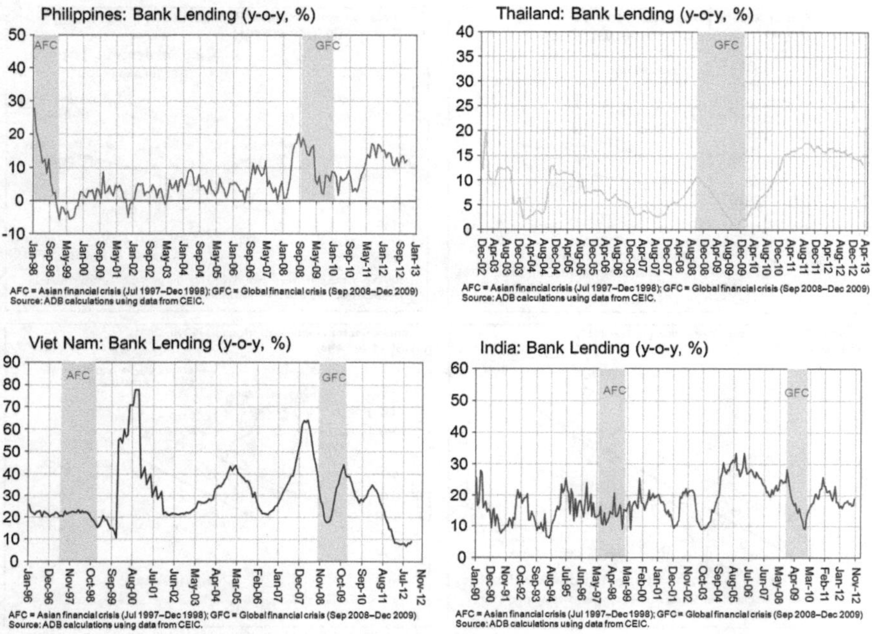

Fig. 2.22 (continued)

It is clear that as banks and other financial institutions expand their liabilities using noncore sources, they tend to diversify their asset holdings by allocating the additional funds either to loans or to other risky financial assets. As a large portion is directed toward the property market and other forms of consumer credit, vulnerabilities multiply. Although the level of noncore liabilities in most economies has yet to set off alarms, it could threaten macro- and financial stability if left unattended.

The attraction for banks holding financial assets has been enhanced by improved liquidity in capital markets as foreign funds flocked to the region. As foreign investors shun risky holdings such as equities, while at the same time seek high risk returns, emerging Asia's LCY bond market has become especially attractive. Asia's safe haven status relative to other developing regions reinforced these flows. The yields of traditionally safer US Treasuries and those of emerging market debt moved in the same direction after the GFC. Slower global growth expectations pushed emerging Asian LCY bond yields lower in tandem with those in advanced economies. This implies that credit risks associated with LCY bonds in the region's emerging markets are significantly lower than in the past.

The share of foreign ownership in some of the region's LCY bond markets has increased, reaching roughly one-third of total bonds outstanding in Indonesia and Malaysia, and more than 10 % in the Republic of Korea and Singapore (Fig. 2.24). Despite this encouraging trend, the relatively small size of emerging Asian LCY

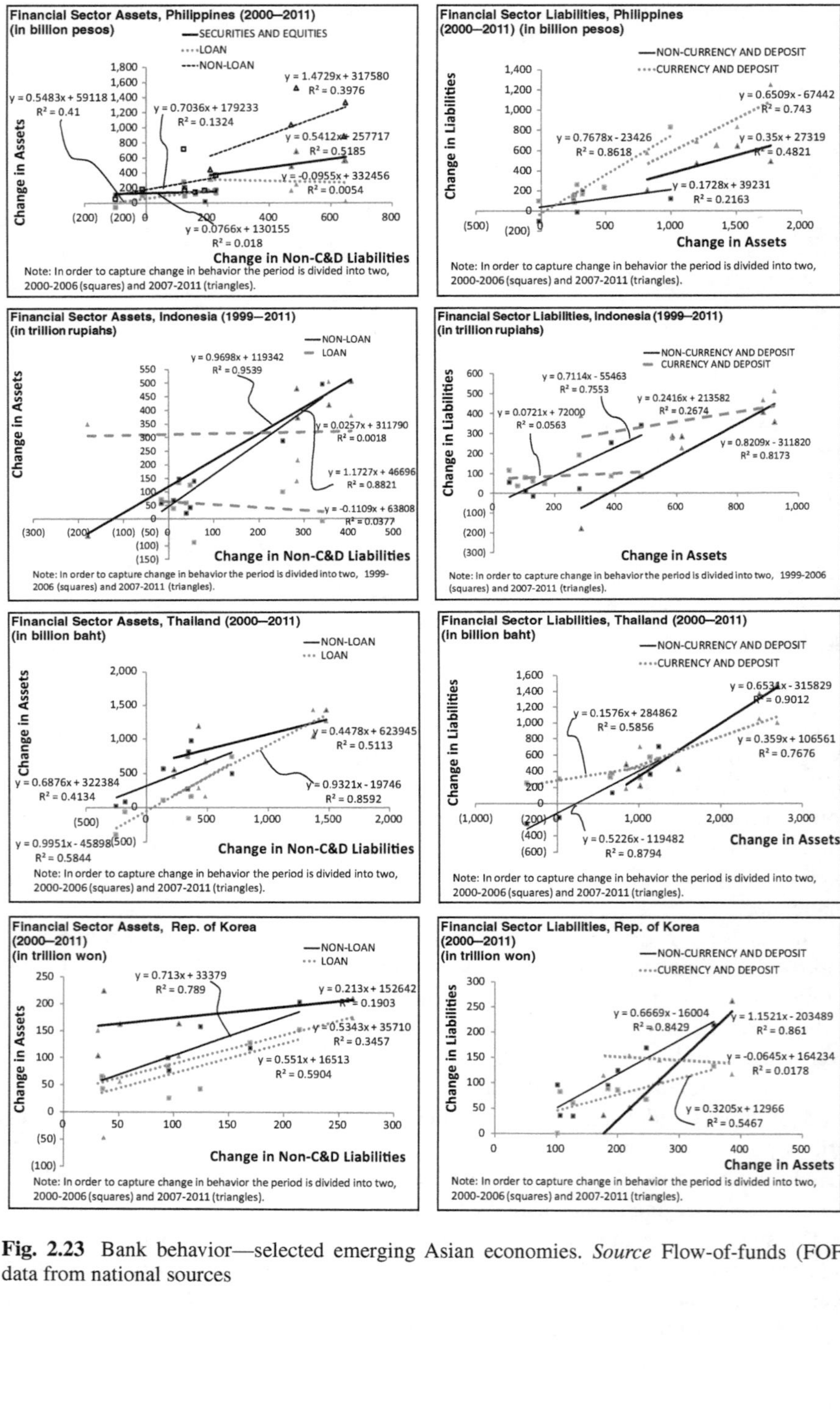

Fig. 2.23 Bank behavior—selected emerging Asian economies. *Source* Flow-of-funds (FOF) data from national sources

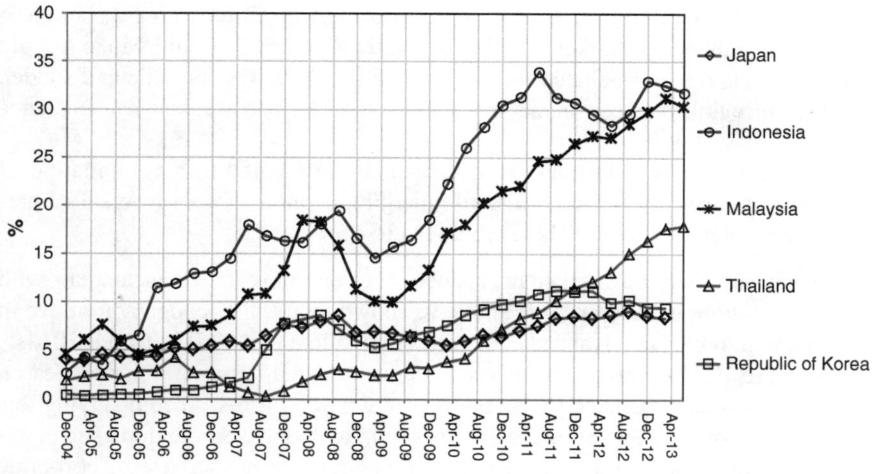

Fig. 2.24 Share of foreign ownership—selected emerging Asian local currency bond markets. *Source* ADB calculations

bond markets and their limited liquidity make these markets sensitive to foreign withdrawals. The resulting volatility can hurt market liquidity and reduce the region's attractiveness to bond investors—as it directly affects investor perceptions of the collateral value of emerging Asian LCY bonds. A recent study by Azis et al. (2013) shows how some Asian markets were significantly affected by US and European bond market volatility associated with both the Lehman failure and Eurozone crisis.

In short, the global flows that fueled capital market liquidity in emerging Asia (second phase) clearly affected the region's financial sector, which is the largest holder of LCY bonds. And with ample liquidity from noncore liabilities (first phase), banks expanded not just lending but their financial assets as well, including LCY sovereign bonds. This has some bearing on the implications for available policy choices.

2.5 Third Phase and Onward

The first and second phases of global liquidity set the stage for a new episode, one that could define a distinct third phase. The Asian experience of capital flow reversals discussed above is particularly relevant in establishing this third phase. The vulnerability caused by bank-led flows through noncore liabilities in the first phase is associated with procyclicality—where a bank's health can deteriorate despite the structural improvements since the Asian financial crisis. While the credit cycle can therefore still be impinged, it is the vulnerability caused by debt-led flows that has become the more pressing concern.

Debt-led flows raised the level of foreign ownership in emerging Asian capital markets, enhancing market liquidity and attracting amply liquid banks to hold financial assets on their balance sheets. When a shock causes sporadic and sudden outflows, this link between banks and capital markets can weaken bank balance sheets when asset prices fall.

In this way, the second phase of global liquidity has led to a combination of forces that increase the vulnerability of emerging economies to a reversal of permissive financial conditions. There are three elements:

i. Yields on emerging market LCY debt securities have fallen in tandem with those in more mature markets and have shown increasing tendency to move in sync with bonds in advanced economies (Miyajima et al. 2012, Turner 2014).
ii. Offshore FCY corporate bond issuance has created currency mismatches on the consolidated balance sheets of emerging market firms. Accompanying this offshore issuance has been growth in corporate deposits in the domestic banking system that becomes vulnerable to withdrawals in the case of corporate distress.
iii. The growing stock of emerging market corporate debt securities has been absorbed by asset managers—whose main reason for buying them has been the perception of stronger economic fundamentals of emerging markets.

All three elements ignited during mid-2013, placing financial markets in emerging economies under severe stress.

The shock that led to the capital outflows was the 22 May 2013 remarks by the US Fed Chairman on the possibility of QE tapering and the subsequent suggestion that the tapering could start in late 2013 and be completed by mid-2014. The remarks sparked a sell-off in bond markets in the US, with bond yields rising from 2.13 % at the beginning of June to 2.74 % on 8 July. Interest rates eased a bit following the US Fed's clarification that the start of tapering was not imminent and would depend on economic conditions. But the bond market sell-off spreads to emerging markets nonetheless, with an immediate impact of rising bond yields, higher interbank rates, and depreciating currencies—albeit the impacts were not felt evenly across all economies.

From May to August 2013, capital outflows from emerging Asia's top 10 economies were estimated at $86 billion, half of which comprised outflows from the PRC. This is still relatively small compared with the $2.1 trillion of inflows between November 2008 and April 2013, an estimate based on foreign exchange reserves data. Between June and August, foreign investors withdrew roughly $19 billion from Asian LCY bond markets. Given the small market size in some economies, the impact was inevitable and significant, especially where the fundamentals were weak (e.g., those with high fiscal and current account deficits). India and Indonesia are notable examples where policy choices became more limited.

In 2013Q2, while there were four emerging Asian economies with current account deficits, only India and Indonesia also had fiscal deficits in 2012 (Table 2.1). Among the 11 economies listed, they also had the two lowest ratios of foreign exchange reserves to GDP and the two highest rates of inflation. As risk

Table 2.1 Vulnerability indicators

	Fiscal balance (% GDP)		Current account (% GDP)		Reserves less gold (% GDP)		Short-term external debt/reserves		Inflation (%)	
	1996	2012	1997Q2[2]	2013Q2[3]	1997Q2	2013Q1	1997Q2	2012Q4	June 1997	Latest[4]
People's Republic of China	−1.8	−1.6	0.8	2.3	13.5	40.7	28.8	12.4	2.8	2.7
Hong Kong, China	2.1	3.2	–	−1.9	39.9	114.2	280.6	65.3	5.5	6.9
India[1]	−7.0	−6.9	−3.1	−3.6	1.3	15.4	–	54.0	12.2	9.6
Indonesia	1.0	−1.8	−1.8	−4.3	8.6	11.6	191.0	49.0	5.3	8.6
Republic of Korea	0.2	−2.9	−2.1	3.5	6.3	27.4	232.0	44.1	4.0	1.4
Malaysia	0.7	−4.5	−4.4	3.7	24.1	44.9	69.2	25.5	2.2	2.0
Philippines	0.3	−2.3	−4.2	5.3	10.2	27.9	105.5	21.2	5.6	2.5
Singapore	21.3	3.9	20.0	20.0	82.7	92.1	245.4	75.1	1.7	1.8
Taipei,China	−1.4	−1.6	1.5	11.6	30.5	83.9	26.6	12.1	1.8	0.1
Thailand	2.1	−4.1	−7.9	−5.1	17.1	43.7	157.7	15.8	4.4	2.0
Viet Nam	−0.9	−6.9	−8.2	4.6	7.0	19.4	53.3	56.3	2.3	7.3

GDP gross domestic product

[1] For India, latest figures are compared with 1991 (annual), not 1997

[2] Annual 1996 current account as % of GDP data for People's Republic of China; Hong Kong, China; India; Malaysia; the Philippines; Thailand; and Viet Nam

[3] 2012Q4 data for Viet Nam; 2013Q1 data for Hong Kong, China; India; the Republic of Korea; Malaysia; and the Philippines

[4] Refers to July 2013 except Singapore (June 2013)

Source ADB calculations using data from ADB Asian Development Outlook, CEIC, Haver Analytics, and national sources perceptions for both economies increased, they endured the largest capital outflows and sharpest currency depreciations (Fig. 2.25).

Between end-May and end-July, government bond yields in Indonesia rose dramatically—from 145 basis points (bps) and 250 bps—shifting the yield curve upward while simultaneously flattening it. This was expected with the capital outflows and given the large share of foreign ownership in their LCY bond markets. By June, foreign investors had become net sellers, with capital outflows of IDR15.76 trillion during the month. Bond market sentiment was also dampened by warnings from rating agencies of a possible sovereign downgrade. These factors' cumulative effect was to raise borrowing costs, which may have postponed new private sector investments using local markets.

With banks the biggest bondholders in Indonesia, bond market vulnerabilities can damage bank balance sheets (Fig. 2.26). To the extent LCY bond markets are

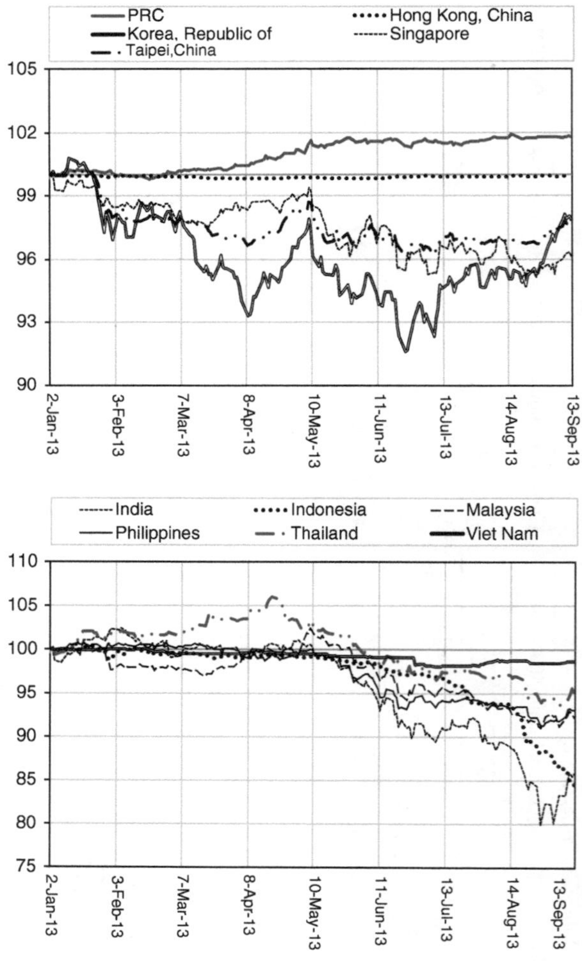

Fig. 2.25 Exchange rate indexes (January 2, 2013 = 100). *PRC* People's Republic of China. *Notes* 1. Spot market exchange rates are quoted as $ per unit of local currency. 2. An increase means appreciation; a decrease means depreciation. *Source* ADB calculations using data from Datastream

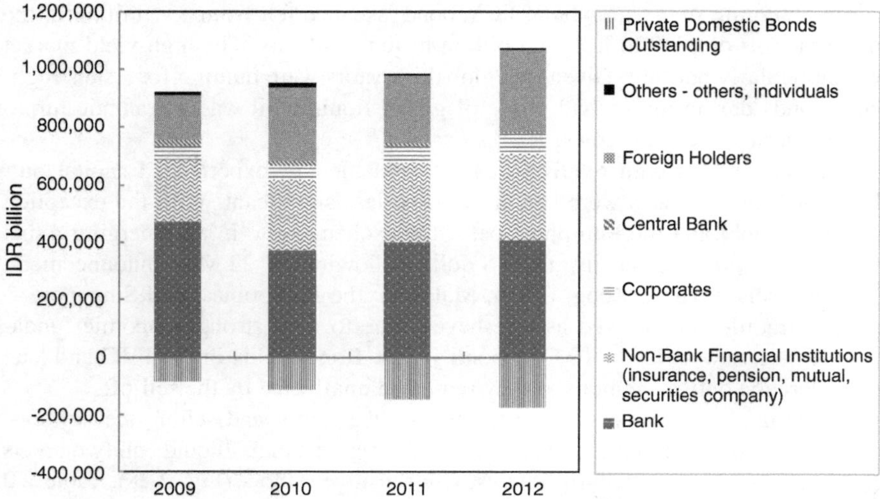

Fig. 2.26 Outstanding bond holdings by investor versus private domestic debt issuance in Indonesia. *Source* AsiaBondsOnline

Fig. 2.27 G3 currency bond issuance. *G3* Eurozone, Japan, US. *Note* G3 currency bond issuance covers data for the People's Republic of China; Hong Kong, China; Indonesia; the Republic of Korea; Malaysia; the Philippines; Singapore; Thailand; and Viet Nam. *Source* ADB calculations based on Bloomberg LP data

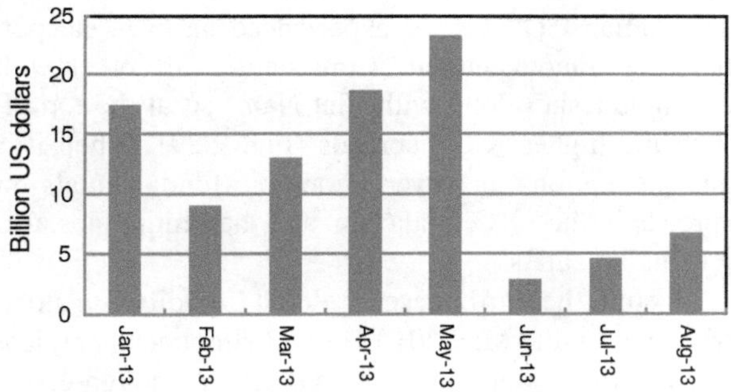

preferred—as they provide a more stable source of long-term funding without the risk of currency mismatch—the trend was not good. However, with its rising fiscal deficit, there was no choice for the Indonesian government but to continue issuing bonds.

Issuing FCY bonds has become more difficult and expensive as well. Issuance of FCY bonds in emerging Asia declined dramatically in June 2013 and only slightly recovered in subsequent months (Fig. 2.27). Although the figure leaves out India, the world's third largest economy, the same thing happened—Indian firms' overseas bond sales slowed significantly.[5] Only one Indian company (Indian Oil) managed to sell a US$-denominated bond during the period after 22 May when the US Fed hinted at QE tapering.

[5] Third largest in PPP terms.

For emerging Asia as a whole, FCY bond issuance fell from $81 billion in the first 5 months of 2013 to just $7.5 billion in June and July. The high-yield market was particularly hard hit. Given that global investors were hunting for Asia's high-yield bonds during the second phase of global liquidity, it was a dramatic turnaround in terms of capital flows.

Even economies with relatively sound fundamentals experienced capital outflows—US market risks were perceived to be less significant. With the exception of the renminbi and the Philippine peso, the exchange rate in all emerging Asian economies depreciated against the US dollar following the 22 May announcement. Bond markets in Hong Kong, China; Malaysia; the Philippines; and Singapore—markets traditionally viewed as safe havens due to their strong economic fundamentals—all saw a rise in 10-year bond yields. Bond yields in the PRC and Viet Nam were the only exceptions as they remained unaffected by the sell-off.

Equity market investors—prone to "buying the rumor and selling the news"—also began to bail. Asset price swings reflect the region's thin, illiquid equity markets as prices jumped, especially in interest-rate-sensitive sectors (Fig. 2.28). Table 2.2 summarizes the direction and magnitude of changes in bond yields, credit default swap (CDS) spreads, equity markets, and exchange rates since 22 May.

With rising capital outflows, weakening capital markets, and depreciated exchange rates, market confidence fell—indicated by rising CDS spreads, which increased almost 60 bps in Indonesia from the beginning of April to end-July. The Indian CDS spread experienced an even steeper increase following the QE tapering announcement. Consistent with other vulnerability indicators, India and Indonesia (along with Viet Nam) sit at the top of emerging Asian economies with the highest CDS spreads (Fig. 2.29). When it comes to market confidence and perceptions, however, economic fundamentals may take the back seat. CDS spreads in the PRC, Malaysia, and the Philippines also increased despite their better fundamentals.

In sum, the third phase of global liquidity is a story about capital flow reversals triggered by the May 2013 US Fed announcement, leading to elevated risk perceptions toward emerging Asian markets. Although economies with weak fundamentals were hit hardest, outflows occurred across the board. The repercussions for capital markets and exchange rates, however, were varied.

When global financial conditions eventually tighten—as the US Fed begins to raise rates—vulnerabilities will likely impact market behavior yet again. Given the elements underpinning the second phase of global liquidity, the crisis dynamics in the emerging economies would then have the following elements:

Step 1. Steepening of the LCY yield curve
Step 2. Currency depreciation, corporate distress, and runs of wholesale corporate deposits from the domestic banking system
Step 3. Decline in corporate capital expenditure directly feeding into slowing economic growth
Step 4. Asset managers cutting back positions in emerging market corporate bonds, citing the slower growth, and
Step 5. A return to Step 1, completing the loop

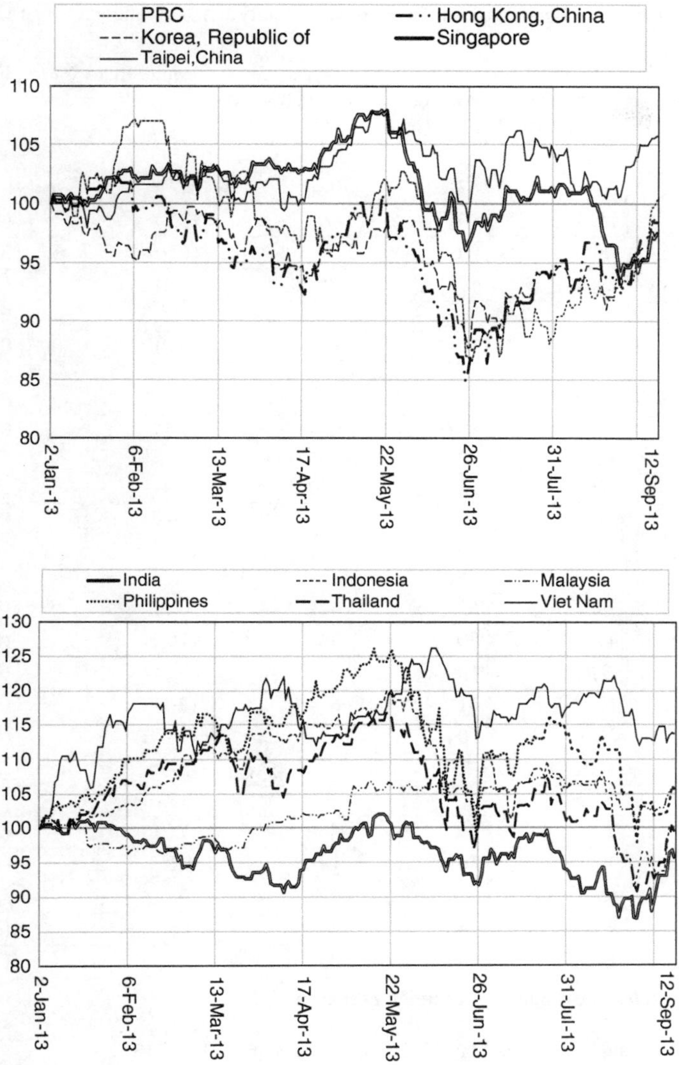

Fig. 2.28 Stock Price Index (January 2, 2013 = 100), *Notes* 1. For the People's Republic of China (*PRC*), daily stock price indexes are the combined Shanghai and Shenzhen composites, weighted by market capitalization in US dollars. 2. Data as of September 12, 2013. *Source* ADB calculations using data from Bloomberg

The distress dynamics sketched above holds some unfamiliar elements. We normally invoke either leverage or maturity mismatches when explaining crises—with the usual protagonists in the crisis narrative banks or other financial intermediaries. In contrast, in this pending scenario, asset managers are at its heart. We find this unsettling, as long- or hold-to-maturity investors are meant to be benign, not add to market vulnerability—they are routinely excluded from the list of "systemic" market participants.

Table 2.2 Changes in bond markets, CDS spreads, equity markets, and exchange rates—since May 22, 2013

	2-year government bond (bps)	10-year government bond (bps)	5-year credit default swap spread (bps)	Equity index (%)	FX rate (%)
Major advanced economies					
US	20	87	0	1.7	–
UK	15	104	(7)	(3.7)	(5.0)
Japan	(1)	(16)	(1)	(6.9)	3.5
Germany	23	57	(0.3)	(0.4)	(3.4)
Emerging Asia					
People's Republic of China	90	70	11	(2.0)	0.2
Hong Kong, China	21	127	9	(1.3)	0.1
India	169	133	150	(1.4)	(14.5)
Indonesia	315	290	110	(16.3)	(16.2)
Republic of Korea	19	60	4	0.5	2.6
Malaysia	29	67	47	(0.6)	(8.5)
Philippines	49	70	35	(16.1)	(6.4)
Singapore	(3)	100	0	(9.6)	(0.1)
Taipei,China	16	41	6	(2.1)	0.3
Thailand	26	104	42	(14.3)	(6.0)
Viet Nam	100	(25)	–	(5.3)	(0.5)
Select European markets					
Greece	2	99	0	(7.7)	(3.4)
Ireland	40	56	18	4.1	(3.4)
Italy	65	61	6	(0.1)	(3.4)
Portugal	219	188	247	0.6	(3.4)
Spain	18	28	23	5.5	(3.4)

– not available, *bps* basis points, *FX* foreign exchange

Notes

1. Data reflect changes between May 22, 2013, and September 12, 2013
2. For Emerging Asia, a positive (negative) value for the FX rate indicates the appreciation (depreciation) of the local currency against the US dollar
3. For European markets, a positive (negative) value for the FX rate indicates the depreciation (appreciation) of the local currency against the US dollar. *Source* Bloomberg LP, Institute of International Finance (IIF), and Thomson Reuters

However, the distinction between leveraged institutions and these long-term investors matters less if they share the same tendency toward procyclicality. Asset managers are answerable to the trustees of the fund that gives them their mandate. In turn, the trustees are themselves agents vis-à-vis the ultimate

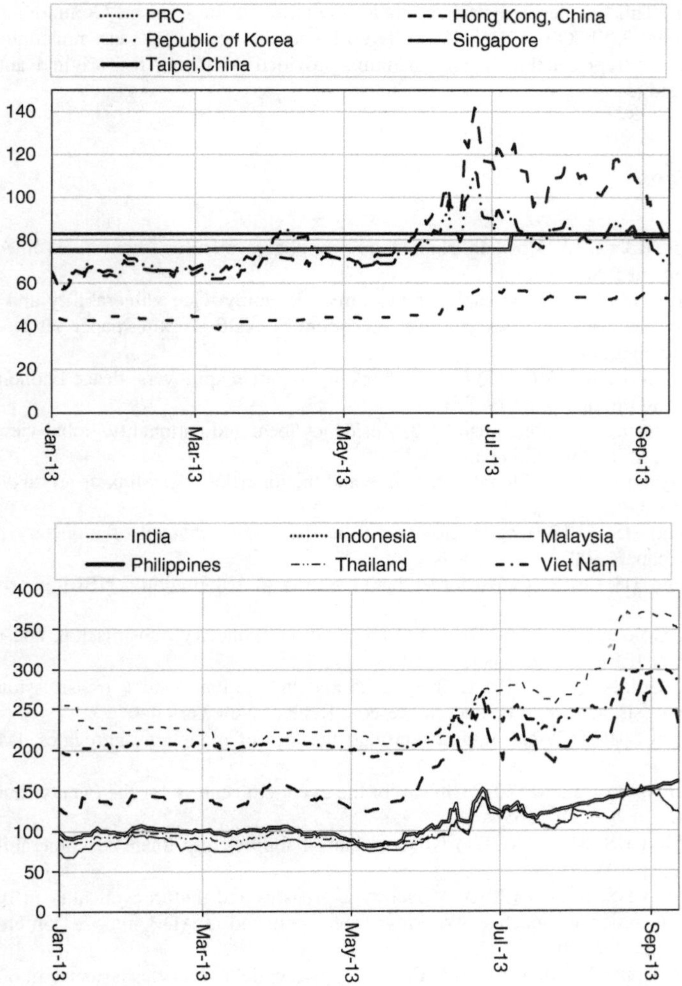

Fig. 2.29 Credit default swap spreads—selected Asian economies. *PRC* People's Republic of China. *Note* Data as of September 12, 2013. *Source* Datastream

beneficiaries. In this way, asset managers lie at the end of a chain of principal–agent relationships that may induce restrictions on their discretion in selecting their portfolio. Frequently, trading restrictions are based on measures of risk used by banks and other leveraged players. As such, their behavior could show the same type of procyclical risk-taking that banks are well known for. The uncomfortable lesson is that asset managers may not conform to the textbook picture of long-term investors, but instead may have much more in common with banks in amplifying shocks.

References

Azis IJ, Shin HS (2013) How do global liquidity phases manifest themselves in Asia? Asian Development Bank, Manila

Azis IJ, Yarcia D (2014) How capital flows affect economy-wide vulnerability and inequality: flow-of-funds analysis of selected Asian economies. ADB working paper series on regional economic integration 136

Azis IJ, Mitra S, Baluga A (2013) Global shock and regional spillovers. Peace Economics, Peace Science and Public Policy 19(2):1–29

Bank for International Settlements (2012) Residency/local and nationality/global views of financial positions. IFC working paper 8

Borio C, Disyatat P (2011) Global imbalances and the financial crisis: link or no link? BIS working papers 346

Bruno V, Shin HS (2012) Capital flows and the risk-taking channel of monetary policy. BIS working papers 400

Bruno V, Shin HS (2013) Cross-border banking, and global liquidity. NBER working papers 19038

Cetorelli N, Goldberg L (2008) Banking globalization, monetary transmission, and the lending channel. NBER working papers 14101

Cetorelli N, Goldberg L (2010) Global banks and international shock transmission: evidence from the crisis, staff reports, Federal Reserve Bank of New York 446

Chung K et al (2013) Global liquidity through the lens of monetary aggregates. IMF working paper 14/9

Gourinchas PO, Obstfeld M (2012) Stories of the twentieth century for the twenty-first. Am Econ J Macroecon 4(1):226–265

Hahm JH, Shin HS, Shin K (2011) Noncore bank liabilities and financial vulnerability. NBER working paper W18428

Hahm JH, Shin HS, Shin K (2013) Monetary aggregates and the procyclicality of the financial system: an Asian perspective. Working paper presented at ADB interim conference, Hong Kong, China, Jan 2013

McCauley R, Upper C, Villar A (2013) Emerging market debt securities issuance in offshore centres. BIS Q Rev Sept

Miyajima K, Mohanty MS, Chan T (2012) Emerging market local currency bonds: diversification and stability. BIS working papers 391

Schularick M, Taylor A (2012) Credit booms gone bust: monetary policy, leverage cycles, and financial crises, 1870–2008. Am Econ Rev 102:1029–1061

Shin HS (2012) Global banking glut and loan risk premium. Mundell-Fleming lecture. IMF Econ Rev 60(2):155–192

Shin HS, Zhao Y (2013) Monetary aggregates and global liquidity: evidence from individual firm data from Asia. Working paper presented at ADB interim conference, Hong Kong, China, Jan 2013

Turner P (2014) The global long-term interest rate, financial risks and policy choices in EMEs. BIS working paper 441

Chapter 3
Early Warning Indicators for Financial Vulnerabilities

This chapter considers the principles underlying the design and implementation of early warning indicators. We argue that indicators based on quantities—especially balance sheet aggregates—are most likely to yield indicators that issue warning signals well before vulnerabilities have grown too large for policy makers to control. As shown in Chap. 2, during the first phase of global liquidity, noncore liabilities of financial intermediaries were most likely to yield timely signals—as banks were center stage in intermediating credit growth. The second phase of global liquidity pivoted on the behavior of capital markets, so the behavior of fund managers should be reflected in the indicator. When credit growth is driven by corporate bond issuance by nonfinancial borrowers, aggregate issuance by corporates would be a useful indicator. In addition, if corporate borrowers engage in "carry trades" by borrowing in foreign currency (FCY) while holding the proceeds of corporate bond issuance in local currency financial instruments and deposits, then tracking the aggregate cash holdings of corporates would also yield useful information.

3.1 Principles for Selection of Early Warning Indicators

Finding a set of early warning indicators that can signal vulnerability to financial turmoil has always been a policy priority in emerging economies. In the aftermath of the global financial crisis, however, it has also become a paramount policy goal for advanced economies. There is ample literature on early warning indicators for financial crises, well described in a recent International Monetary Fund (IMF) survey (Chamon and Crowe 2012). Crises in emerging economies during the 1990s ignited much of the work. For example, in their overview of the literature as of 1998, Kaminsky et al. (1998) catalogued 105 variables that had been used until then. But the search deepened in the aftermath of the global financial crisis.

I.J. Azis and H.S. Shin, *Managing Elevated Risk*,
DOI 10.1007/978-981-287-284-5_3

Here, we review the principles behind the selection of early warning indicators based on Shin (2013). The conventional approach was to distinguish between crises in emerging economies from those in advanced economies—with a different set of variables for each group. For example, emerging economy crises focus on capital flow reversals associated with "sudden stops," where variables such as external borrowings denominated in FCY take center stage. For advanced economies, housing booms and household leverage were more important. This distinction is also reflected in the work of official multilateral institutions. The IMF has added a new vulnerability exercise for advanced economies (VEA) to an existing vulnerability exercise for emerging economies (VEE), which both feed into a joint early warning exercise with the Financial Stability Board (FSB).

Although the split between emerging and advanced economies helps improve the "goodness of fit," it tends to obscure common threads underlying both types of crises. Capital flow reversals in Spain and Ireland during the Eurozone crisis mimic many features of a "sudden stop," except that private sector fund outflows have been compensated for by the inflow of official funds. However, since the Eurozone crisis occurred in a common currency area, the traditional classification of emerging market "currency crises"—where currency movements play a key role—does not fit easily in an empirical exercise.

Given the common threads that tie together apparently disparate crises, it is useful to step back from the practical imperative of maximizing goodness of fit and instead consider the conceptual underpinnings of early warning models. The guiding theme here is that the procyclicality of the financial system provides an organizing framework for selecting vulnerability indicators, especially those associated with banks and financial intermediaries more generally.

To set the stage for our study, we consider the three broad sets of indicators for early warning purposes and assess their relative likelihood of success.

i. Indicators based on market prices, such as credit default swap (CDS) spreads, implied volatility, and other price-based measures of default or distress;
ii. Gap measures of the credit-to-GDP ratio; and
iii. Banking sector liability aggregates, including monetary aggregates.

The first approach (based on market prices) seems most appropriate for obtaining indicators of concurrent market conditions. But it is less useful in identifying early warning indicators with enough lead time for meaningful remedial action. The credit-to-GDP gap measure is a distinct improvement from the first. It boasts good pedigree from the work of economists at the Bank for International Settlements (BIS). And it has been explored extensively as part of the Basel III bank capital rules. However, some authors raise questions on the real-time properties of the credit-to-GDP measure.

The third approach—based on bank liability aggregates—rests on the same principles as credit measures. To the extent measures of bank liabilities also convey information on the size of consolidated bank balance sheets, they may be useful as a measure of financial vulnerability. As a measurement exercise, the balance sheet of the entire banking sector can be measured either in terms of assets or in terms of liabilities, which may show different dynamics from the interest rates that most research tracks. Nevertheless, bank liabilities tend to be more transparent and homogenous than bank assets. Liabilities tend to be short term—mainly in the form of deposits—and hence, their book values are close to marked-to-market values. In addition, liabilities are more easily organized into core and noncore liabilities with contrasting cyclical properties. Noncore liabilities exhibit greater procyclicality, so the ratio of noncore to core liabilities provides useful information as an early warning indicator of financial vulnerability (Hahm et al. 2013).

One consequence of the monetary approach is that any measure derived this way will need to fit the specific institutional features of the financial system, rather than being applied universally in an unthinking way. These institutional details turn out to matter quite a lot. So for example, the People's Republic of China would need to heed quite different details of its financial system than, say, the Republic of Korea, which has a more open banking sector. One of the tasks is to set out a broader conceptual framework that allows us to encompass the different cases and to lay out the principles for when indicators should be used and under what circumstances.

Along with heeding institutional differences, we also need to transcend traditional thinking behind the definitions of monetary aggregates to make the approach useful. Whereas traditional definitions of monetary aggregates exclude liabilities between financial intermediaries, liability aggregates are perhaps the most informative of them all.

Before exploring the attributes of bank liability aggregates, we first discuss the relative merits of the three approaches to early warning indicators mentioned above.

Figure 3.1 shows the CDS spreads of Bears Stearns and Lehman Brothers, with the right-hand panel giving the longer term perspective and illustrating how these spreads increased sharply with the onset of the crisis.

It is remarkable how tranquil the CDS measure was before the crisis. There was barely a ripple in the series between 2004 and 2006, when vulnerability to financial crisis was building. The left-hand panel plots the CDS series for the precrisis period between January 2004 and January 2007. It shows that CDS spreads were

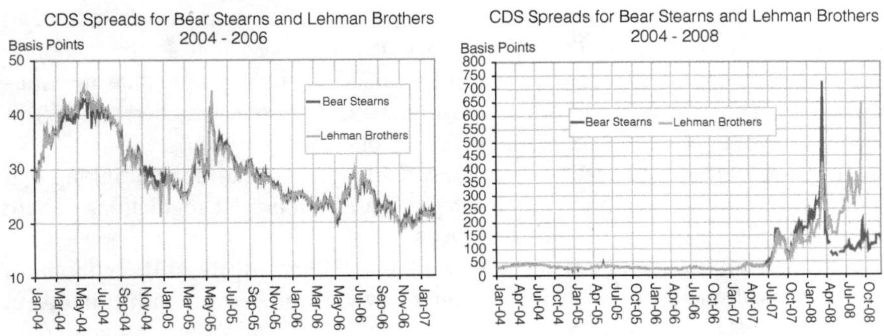

Fig. 3.1 Credit default swap (CDS) spreads for Bear Stearns and Lehman Brothers. *Note Left panel* 2004–2006, *Right panel* 2004–2008. *Source* Bankscope

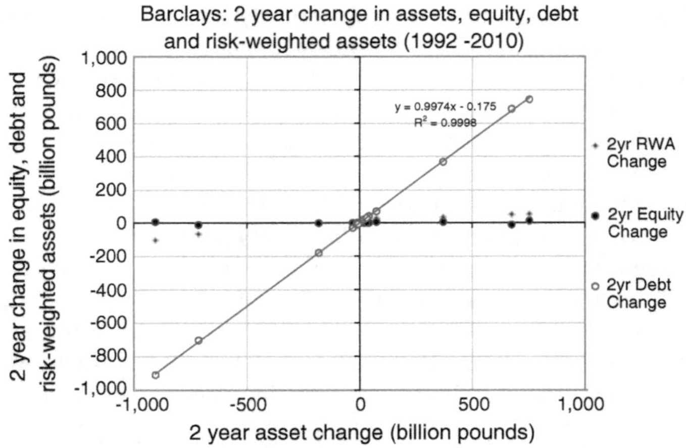

Fig. 3.2 Changes in assets versus changes in debt, equity, and risk-weighted assets of Barclays (1992–2010). *Source* Bankscope

actually falling, dipping below 20 basis points at the end of 2006. Other price-based measures, such as value-at-risk, implied volatility; structural models of default based on equity prices, among others, all paint the same picture.

The failure of price-based measures as early warning indicators can be traced to the implicit premise that market signals and decisions guided by those signals always interact in a stabilizing virtuous circle. Rather, they sometimes go astray and act together to amplify a vicious circle instead, where market signals and decisions made reinforce an existing tendency toward procyclicality.

To illustrate this, a scatter chart plots how much the change in balance sheet size of Barclays—a typical global bank—is financed through equity and how much through debt (Fig. 3.2). It also shows how risk-weighted assets changed as the balance sheet grows or shrinks.

The fact that risk-weighted assets barely increase—even as raw assets are increasing rapidly—is indicative of how measured risks (such as spreads or value-at-risk measures) move lower during lending booms. Lower measured risks and lending booms thus go together. The reverse causation also holds—the compression of risk spreads is induced by the rapid increase in credit supply chasing available credit. This two-way causation builds a feedback loop in which greater credit supply and the compression of spreads feed off one another.

This amplified procyclicality poses hard challenges for traditional thinking that puts faith in market discipline as an integral part of financial regulation—where prices are relied on to issue timely warning signals.

Indeed, market discipline was one of the three "Pillars" of Basel II. Economists associated with the Shadow Financial Regulatory Committee were influential here. Calomiris (1999) argued for rules requiring banks to maintain a minimum amount of subordinated debt, the rationale being that banks that take on excessive risk find it difficult to sell their subordinated debt. Thus, they will be forced to shrink risky assets or issue new equity to comply with the discipline imposed by private uninsured creditors. However, the run-up to the recent crisis showed just how market risk premiums erode so as to nullify market discipline.

Larry Summers's quip (Summers 1985) that finance researchers need to show that "two-quart bottles of ketchup invariably sell for twice as much as one-quart bottle of ketchup" is related to the reason why price-based measures of early warning indicators will likely fail. Absence of arbitrage means that prices at a point in time are consistent, but they are liable to flip into distress mode (again, fully consistent across assets) with the onset of a crisis. If the task is to give prior warning of the onset of a crisis, price-based measures have little to say.

As the start of a crisis is often accompanied by a panicked run to the exits, the switch from a benign environment to a hostile one can be precipitous indeed. Global games literature illustrates how the transition into financial distress—the "tipping point"—is associated with self-reinforcing effects between individual constraints and market outcomes; how the onset of a crisis is triggered by apparently small changes in underlying fundamentals. Outwardly, the switch into crisis is almost self-fulfilling. Goldstein (2010) discusses how empirical research should take account of tipping points and shows how the global games framework (Morris and Shin 1998, 2001, 2008) is useful in a modeling exercise.

Market prices have been useful for early warning exercises precisely when the market price of risk is too low, rather than too high. Thus, it is when asset prices are too high relative to some benchmark that warnings are appropriate.

In their 2005 paper on the US housing market, Himmelberg et al. (2005) argued that a high price-to-rent ratio or high price-to-income ratio need not predicate a housing bubble—as discount rates implied by low long-term interest rates had also fallen. But as discount rates are prices, the combination of low discount rates and high housing prices is arguably the kind of point-in-time consistency in prices that Summers (1985) had in mind.

Under Basel III, the ratio of credit to GDP takes a central role as the basis for the countercyclical capital buffer. As shown by Borio and Lowe (2002, 2004), this ratio is useful as an indicator of the stage of the financial cycle. To the extent procyclicality drives financial vulnerability, detecting excessive credit growth is central. Normalizing credit to some underlying fundamental measure such as GDP—and detecting deviations from trend—would be one way to operationalize the notion of excessive credit growth.

However, although a credit boom is clear with hindsight, there are several challenges in using the deviation from trend of credit-to-GDP ratios as an early warning indicator in real time.

The first is the difficulty of estimating the trend that serves as benchmark for what is considered "excessive" growth. The difficulty is not unique to the credit-to-GDP ratio—it is shared by other macroeconomic time series. Edge and Meisenzahl (2011) find that ex post revisions to the credit-to-GDP ratio gap in real time are sizable for the US and as large as the gap itself. The source of the ex post revisions is not the revision of underlying data, but rather from the revision of the estimated trend measured in real time.

The second difficulty is that credit growth and GDP dance to somewhat different tunes over the cycle, so that the ratio of the two may sometimes issue misleading signals. Bank lending in particular may be influenced by preexisting contractual commitments, such as lines of credit, which are drawn down during a crisis. Ivashina and Scharfstein (2010) document the impact of lines of credit on credit growth during the recent crisis. Therefore, lending may continue to increase for some time after the onset of the crisis.

Repullo and Saurina (2011) show the credit-to-GDP ratio for the UK and its Hodrick–Prescott (HP)-filtered trend (Fig. 3.3). The HP filter parameter is set at $\lambda = 400{,}000$ as recommended by the Basel Committee, which effectively means a linear trend. The bottom panel shows the credit-to-GDP ratio "gap" between the credit-to-GDP ratio and the trend.

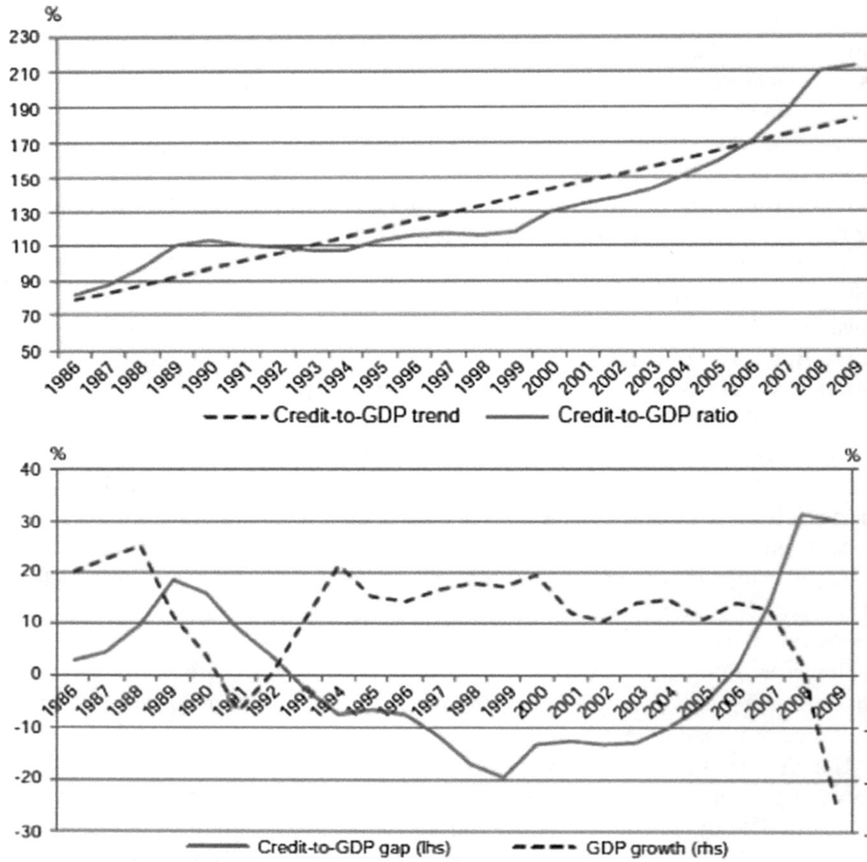

Fig. 3.3 Credit-to-GDP ratio and GDP growth—UK. *GDP* gross domestic product. *Note Top panel* shows UK credit-to-GDP ratio and its time trend (HP filter $\lambda = 40{,}000$), *bottom panel* shows credit-to-GDP gap and GDP growth. *Source* Repullo and Saurina (2011)

From the bottom panel, we note the gap measure is large even as GDP growth is falling sharply during the crisis. Thus, the ratio of the two gives a misleadingly large credit-to-GDP ratio during the crisis.

Basel III discussions give much prominence to the credit-to-GDP gap measure (BCBS 2009, 2010). To the extent the Basel rules are expected to be applied uniformly (or at least consistently), finding common thresholds for the credit-to-GDP ratio would be a basic requirement if Basel III is to apply uniformly to all Basel Committee member countries.

3.2 Core and Noncore Liabilities

In addressing financial system procyclicality, it is useful to distinguish between banks' core and noncore liabilities. Core liabilities are the funds banks draw on during normal times and are sourced (in the main) domestically. What constitutes core funding depends on the context and the economy in question, but retail household deposits would be a good first conjecture in defining core liabilities.

When bank assets grow rapidly, the core funding available will likely be insufficient to finance the rapid credit growth. This is because retail deposits grow in line with the aggregate wealth of households. In a lending boom, when credit is growing very rapidly, the pool of retail deposits will likely be insufficient to fund growth in bank credit. Other sources must be tapped. The state of the financial cycle is thus reflected in the composition of bank liabilities.

Banks' procyclical behavior has consequences for capital flows. Banks are intermediaries that borrow in order to lend, and they must raise funding in order to lend to their borrowers. When credit is expanding rapidly, outstripping the pool of available retail deposits, the bank will turn to other sources of funding to support credit growth, typically from other banks operating as wholesale lenders in the capital market. Here, there are close parallels between currency crises and credit crises. The link comes from the fact that the procyclical behavior of banks fueling the credit boom is financed through capital inflows entering via the banking sector. Indeed, one of the key results of our empirical investigation below is that the most consistently reliable indicator of vulnerability for both currency and credit crises is a high level of foreign bank liabilities.

By addressing the up-phase of the financial cycle—and the potential for the compression of risk premiums during lending booms—our approach differs from models of leverage constraints or collateral constraints that bind only during the downturn. In these models, lending is always below the first best. As well as the downturn, our focus is on the up-phase of the cycle when risk premiums become compressed, leaving the economy vulnerable to a potential reversal.

Figure 3.4 is a schematic illustration of the buildup of vulnerabilities associated with the growth of noncore liabilities. The bottom panel is the banking sector before a credit boom, while the top panel illustrates the system after the boom. As traditional deposit funding does not keep up with credit growth, the banking

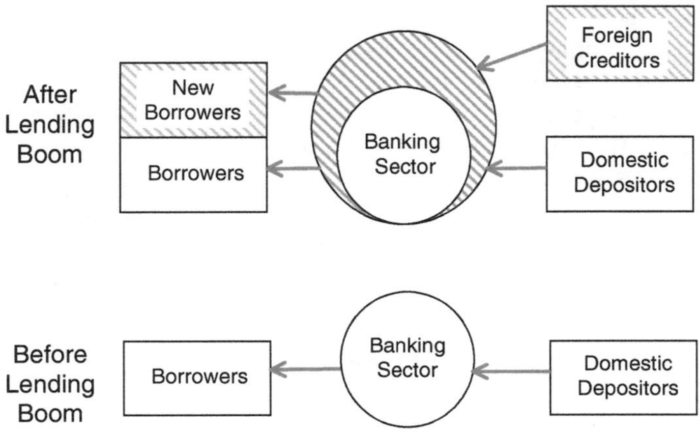

Fig. 3.4 Lending boom financed by noncore liabilities. *Note* Increased lending during a credit boom is financed by noncore liabilities. *Source* Authors' illustration

sector's expansion is funded by noncore liabilities (in this case, from foreign creditors), building vulnerabilities to foreign creditor deleveraging.

Two features distinguish noncore liabilities. First, they include claims held by intermediaries on other intermediaries. And second, they include liabilities to foreign creditors, who are typically global banks, and hence also intermediaries, if foreign ones. Even for liabilities to domestic creditors, if the creditor is another intermediary, the claim tends to be short term. The distinction between core and noncore liabilities becomes meaningful once there are differences in the empirical properties of the two types of liabilities.

Where the line between core and noncore liabilities lies depends very much on the financial system in question, its degree of openness, and stage of financial market and institutional development. For a developed financial system, as in the US or western Europe, the distinction between core and noncore liabilities seems reasonably well captured by the distinction between deposit versus nondeposit funding. Figure 3.5, taken from Shin (2009), shows the composition of the liabilities of Northern Rock, the UK bank whose failure in 2007 heralded the global financial crisis.

In the 9 years from 1998 to 2007, Northern Rock's lending increased 6.5 times. This increase in lending far outstripped funds raised through retail deposits, with the rest of the funding gap filled by wholesale funding.

The Northern Rock case illustrates a general lesson—that during a credit boom, the rapid increase in bank lending outstrips the core deposit funding available to a bank. As the boom progresses, the bank resorts to alternative, noncore liabilities to finance lending. Therefore, the proportion of noncore bank liabilities serves as a useful indicator of the stage of the financial cycle and the degree of vulnerability of the banking system to a downturn in that cycle.

For emerging or developing economies, including those in Asia, more thought is needed to find a useful classification system between core and noncore

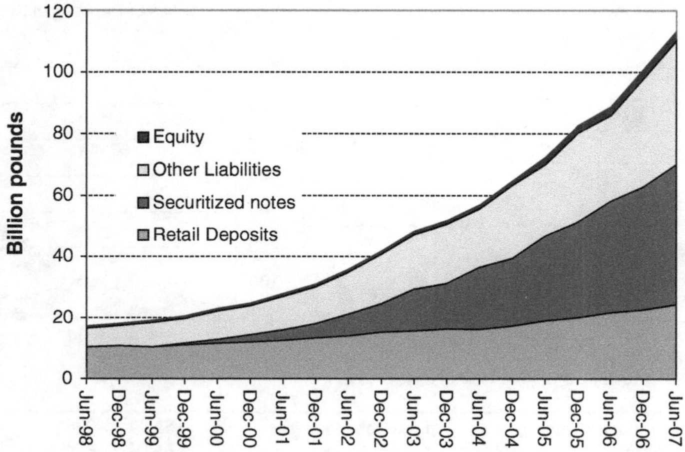

Fig. 3.5 Northern Rock liabilities (1998–2007). *Source* Northern Rock, annual and interim reports, 1998–2007

liabilities. In an open emerging economy where the banking system is open to funding from global banks, rapid increases in noncore bank liabilities show up as capital inflows through increased foreign exchange-denominated banking liabilities. For this reason, foreign exchange-denominated banking liabilities can be expected to play a key role in diagnosing potential financial instability.

For the Republic of Korea, Shin and Shin (2010) proposed a definition of noncore liabilities as the sum of (i) foreign exchange-denominated bank liabilities; (ii) bank debt securities; (iii) promissory notes; (iv) repos; and (v) certificates of deposit (CDs). This measure of noncore liabilities is an approximation of "true" noncore liabilities defined in our accounting framework above, as the classification remains based on financial instruments rather than actual potential claims. For instance, bank debt securities such as debentures and CDs can be held by households, which must be excluded from noncore liabilities.

Figure 3.6 illustrates the situation in the Republic of Korea. The right panel plots six categories of noncore bank liabilities taken from Shin and Shin (2010). It is notable how the first peak in noncore liabilities coincides with the 1997 crisis. After a lull in the early 2000s, noncore liabilities increased rapidly in the run-up to the 2008/2009 crisis.

The left panel plots noncore liabilities as a fraction of broad money (M2) and highlights the highly procyclical nature of noncore liabilities. There is much variation in the ratio of noncore liabilities to M2, ranging from around 15 % of M2 to a peak of 50 % following the bankruptcy of Lehman Brothers, the height of the 2008 global financial crisis.

The pronounced procyclicality of the noncore liability series for the Republic of Korea should not come as a surprise given what we know (from Chap. 2) about how banks manage their balance sheets and the perverse nature of demand and

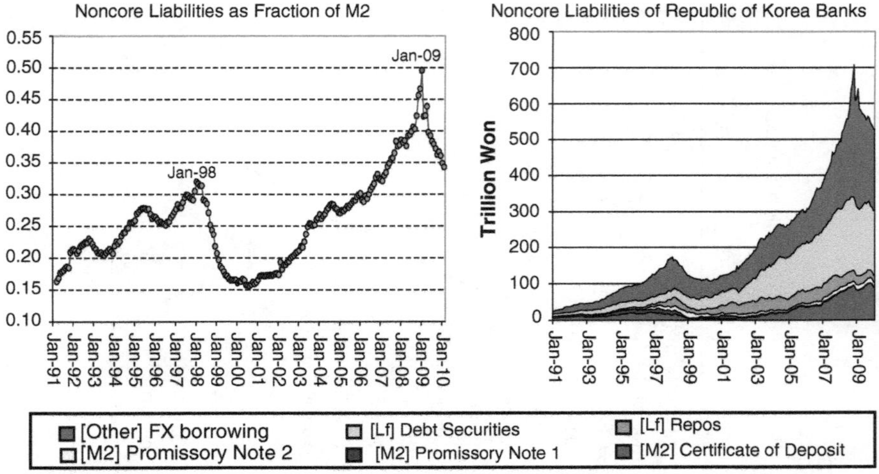

Fig. 3.6 Noncore liabilities of banks—Republic of Korea. *Note Right panel* plots six categories of noncore liabilities of Korean banks measured in Korean won. *Left Panel* plots noncore series as a fraction of broad money (M2). *Source* Bank of Korea and Shin and Shin (2010)

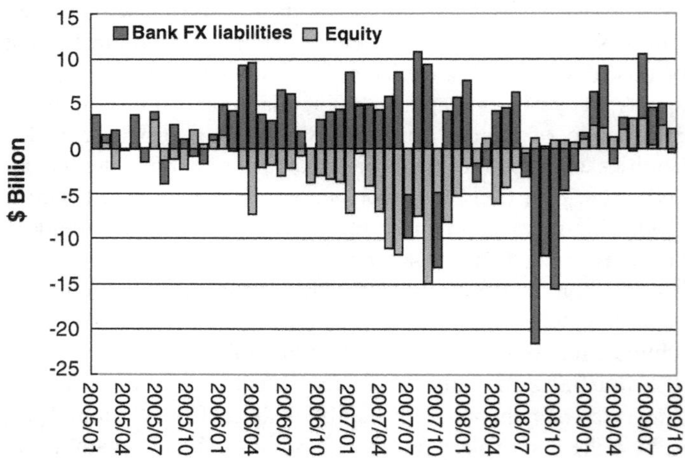

Fig. 3.7 Net capital flows of equity and banking sector. *Source* Shin and Shin (2010)

supply responses to asset price changes and shifts in measured risk. During a credit boom, when measured risks are low and funding from global banks are easy to come by, we would expect to see strong credit growth fueled by capital inflows into the banking sector, often in foreign exchange.

Figure 3.7 shows how capital flows associated with FCY bank liabilities played a key role in the foreign exchange liquidity crisis of 2008 in the Republic of Korea. The figure plots and compares capital inflows and outflows for equities and banks.

During the crisis period in 2008, the equity sector (in light bars) actually received net inflows. Contrary to the common misperception that foreign investors fleeing the Korean stock market were behind the capital outflows (perpetuated by television broadcasts after turbulent trading), net flows in the equity sector were positive immediately after the crisis hit.

There are good reasons why equity markets should see net positive flows during a crisis. Equity outflows are mitigated two ways. During a crisis, not only do stock prices fall sharply, but there is a steep local currency depreciation relative to the US dollar. For both reasons, foreign investors suffer a "double whammy" if they withdraw. Provided the exchange rate is allowed to adjust, equity outflows will not be the main culprit in draining FCY reserves. When Korean investors have equity investments abroad, repatriation flows back will outweigh outflows from foreign investors.

However, the banking sector is different for three reasons. First, FCY liabilities have a face value that must be met in full. Second, the face value is in FCY. And third, the dynamics of deleveraging sets off amplifying effects through price changes and shifts in measured risk.

For all three reasons, bank deleveraging is associated with precipitous capital outflows. Unlike long-term investors such as pension funds, mutual funds, and life insurance companies, leveraged institutions are vulnerable to the erosion of capital and hence substantially adjust their assets even when small shocks strike. The feedback loop generated by these reactions to price changes amplifies the shock.

As Fig. 3.7 shows, the banking sector in the Republic of Korea saw very substantial capital outflows in the aftermath of the crisis. In the three months after the Lehman bankruptcy, banking sector outflows reached $49 billion, which more than accounts for the decrease in the Republic of Korea's foreign exchange reserves—from over $240 billion before the Lehman crisis to $200 billion by the end of 2008. Bank deleveraging and the associated amplification effects figure prominently in emerging economy financial crises.

The sequencing of reforms matters as well. If liberalization of nonfinancial corporate funding proceeds ahead of bank liberalization—as was the case in Japan during the 1980s—it becomes profitable for large manufacturers to recycle liquidity and act as de facto financial intermediaries. They do this by raising funds in capital markets through securities and then depositing the funds in bank time deposits. This can dramatically increase the financial assets of nonfinancial corporations, along with their financial liabilities (Hattori et al. 2009). Figure 3.8 illustrates the change in financial structure that this liquidity recycling entails. When nonfinancial firms act as de facto financial intermediaries, M2 will rise rapidly due to increasing deposit claims on banks. Meanwhile, banks themselves will be under increasing pressure to find new borrowers—as one of their traditional customers (manufacturing firms) no longer needs funding. Instead, banks and manufacturing firms undergo a role reversal, with firms making deposits with banks rather than seeking loans.

When this happens, the distinction between core and noncore bank liabilities does not neatly coincide with the distinction between deposit and nondeposit

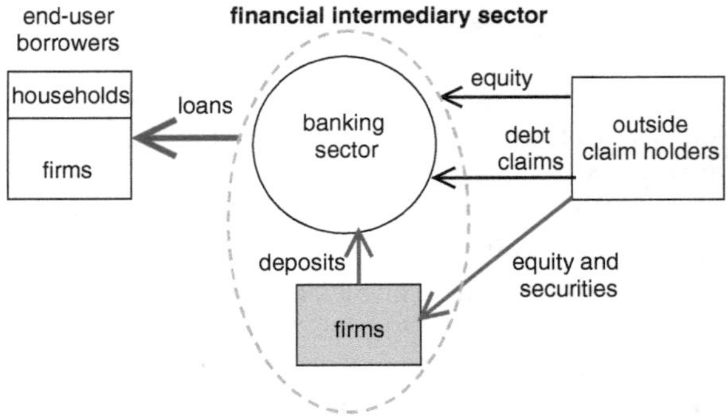

Fig. 3.8 Structural changes in financial intermediation. *Source* Authors' illustration

liabilities. In many developing economies at an early stage of financial development, or in those generally closed to the global banking system, the principle behind the distinction is better expressed as the distinction between retail household deposits and the wholesale deposits of nonfinancial companies.

In practice, however, classifying core and noncore liabilities is not so clear-cut. For small- and medium-sized enterprises (SMEs) with an owner-manager, bank deposits can be seen as household deposits. On the other hand, a firm could have access to market finance and the ability to issue bonds—depositing the proceeds in banks. This is what happened in Japan in the 1980s, for instance. This latter case should not be counted as a core liability as the creditor firm is acting like an intermediary borrowing from financial markets to lend to banks.

Thus, what is considered core or noncore will depend on an economy's financial system and its institutions. For economies with banks operating in developed, open capital markets, noncore funding will typically take the form of wholesale bank funding from capital markets, sometimes denominated in FCY. However, if the economy has a closed capital account with banks prevented from accessing foreign capital market funding, then what is considered noncore funding could be quite different.

A comparison between the PRC and the Republic of Korea helps illustrate this point. Figure 3.9 plots the monthly growth rates of various banking sector liability aggregates for the Republic of Korea (left panel) and the PRC (right panel). The growth rates have been filtered through an HP filter at business cycle frequency. The HP filter is used here with hindsight to highlight differences in time series patterns, as opposed to the real-time, trend-finding exercise under Basel III.

In the Republic of Korea, banks have access to capital markets, either directly or through the foreign bank branches operating in the economy. For this reason, the most procyclical components of bank liability aggregates are those associated with wholesale funding, especially the series for FCY-denominated bank liabilities. The other noncore liabilities are bank debentures, repos, and other nondeposit items such as promissory notes (Shin and Shin 2010). Before the 1997/1998 Asian financial crisis and the global financial crisis, noncore liabilities grew rapidly, only to crash when each crisis begins. In contrast, the growth of M2, reflecting household and corporate deposits, varies much less over the cycle.

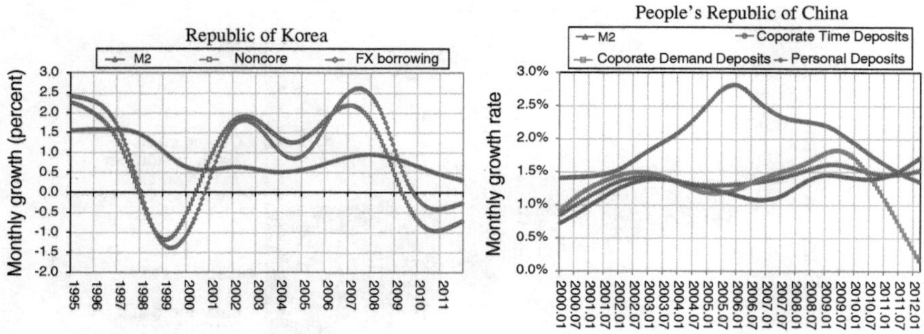

Fig. 3.9 Monthly growth rates of HP-filtered bank liability aggregates—People's Republic of China, Republic of Korea. *Source* Bank of Korea and People's Bank of China

The right panel of Fig. 3.9 shows that in the PRC, the M2 subcomponents exhibit considerable variation in time series properties. For an economy such as the PRC, where banks are prevented from accessing international capital markets, applying the same core and noncore liability classifications as in the Republic of Korea would be inappropriate.

More thought is needed on how financial conditions are transmitted across PRC's border. As mentioned above, just as water finds cracks to flow through, even a closed financial system is not entirely immune to global financial conditions. This is especially true for a highly trade-dependent economy such as the PRC. If banks are prevented from accessing international capital markets, then nonfinancial firms will act as conduit for transmitting financial conditions.

Similar to Fig. 2.16, Fig. 3.10 depicts the activities of a PRC nonfinancial firm with operations outside the country: one that borrows in US dollars from an international bank in Hong Kong, China, and posts renminbi deposits as collateral. The transaction would be akin to a currency swap, except that the settlement price is

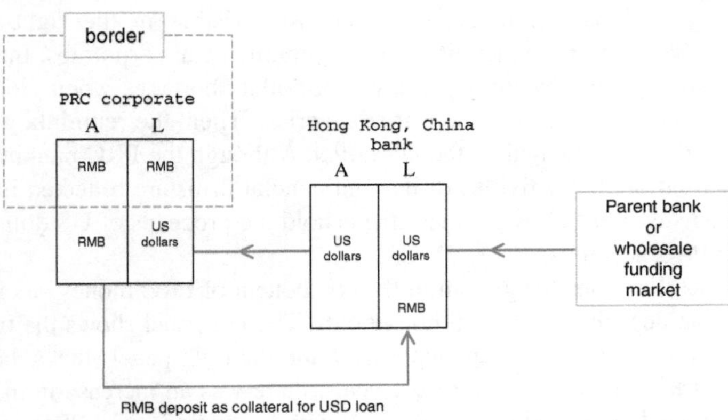

Fig. 3.10 Borrowing relationship structure among nonfinancial corporates in the People's Republic of China. *A* assets; *L* liabilities, *Source* Authors' illustration

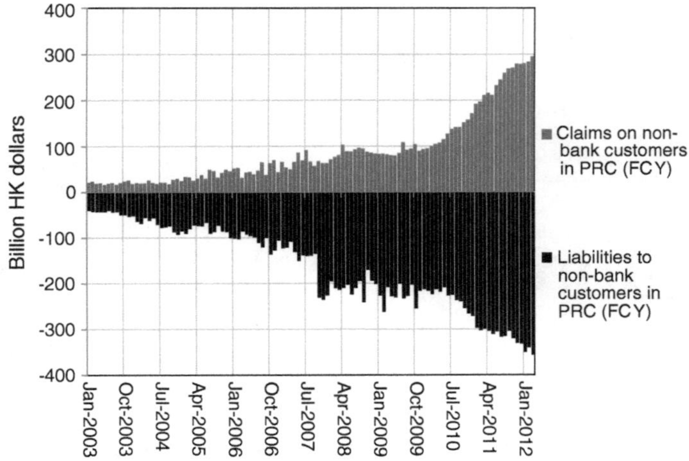

Fig. 3.11 Claims and liabilities of banks in Hong Kong, China, to nonbank customers in the People's Republic of China. *PRC* People's Republic of China, *FCY* foreign currency. *Source* Hong Kong Monetary Authority

decided at the outset. As mentioned earlier, the transactions instead resemble the operation of the old London Eurodollar market in the 1960s and 1970s. For the PRC firm, the purpose of having US dollar liabilities and holding the proceeds in renminbi may be to hedge export receivables or simply to speculate on renminbi appreciation.

Figure 3.11 provides the evidence for the transactions depicted in Fig. 3.9, plotting the FCY claims and liabilities of banks in Hong Kong, China, to customers in the PRC. In this case, the FCY would be (mainly) US dollars for assets and (mainly) renminbi for liabilities. Both have risen dramatically in recent years, reflecting the rapidly rising amount of US dollar funding available to nonfinancial corporates.

The procyclical pattern in corporate deposits visible in the right panel in Fig. 3.9 may be due to these activities among nonfinancial corporates. In addition, they may also explain why the PRC has seen dollar shortages when global funding markets deteriorated due to the Eurozone crisis. Then, the renminbi was under pressure and depreciated against the US dollar. Although the PRC banking system is largely closed, global activities of its nonfinancial firms are reflected in the corporate deposits within M2, when these firms hold the proceeds of US dollar liabilities in their PRC accounts.

Figure 3.12 illustrates the growth in the component of PRC money stock coming from corporate deposits rather than households. The left panel shows the time trend in personal deposits and corporate deposits, while the right panel shows the ratio of corporate to personal deposits. In recent years, there was an increase in the proportion of corporate deposits, which is consistent with the operations of PRC corporates.

The excess liquidity generated by nonfinancial corporate activity in the PRC is an important element of the credit boom. It is reminiscent of the lending boom

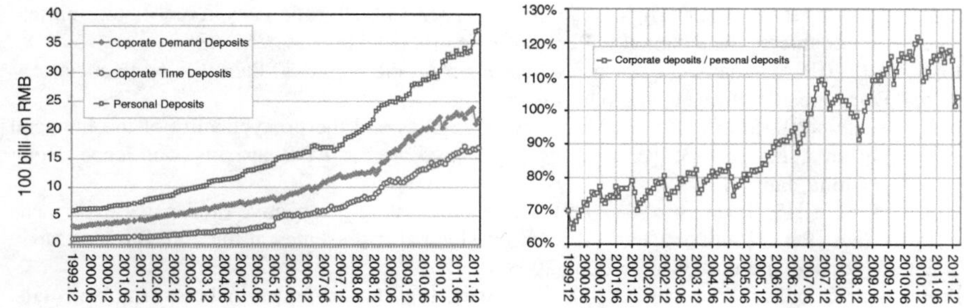

Fig. 3.12 Components of the monetary aggregates—People's Republic of China. *Source* People's Bank of China

in Japan in the 1980s following the financial liberalization that allowed Japanese companies to access global capital markets. Both in Japan in the 1980s and in the PRC more recently, monetary aggregates, especially corporate deposits, played the role of noncore liabilities in the way FCY borrowing by Korean banks played the role of noncore liabilities in the Republic of Korea. The point of contact between FCY liabilities in the Republic of Korea and the corporate deposits in the PRC is that both are bank liabilities.

This points to a broader theme of financialization of nonfinancial companies, where these firms take on attributes of financial firms by increasing the size of their balance sheets relative to their sales-generating activities. As a consequence, they help amplify financial cycles. Therefore, as monetary policy moves from the role of banks to the functioning of bond markets and the availability of credit to borrowers from long-term investors—such as asset managers acting on behalf of pension funds and insurance companies—the role of nonfinancial firms takes on increased significance.

References

Basel Committee on Banking Supervision (2009) Strengthening the resilience of the banking sector. http://www.bis.org/publ/bcbs164.pdf

Basel Committee on Banking Supervision (2010) International regulatory framework for banks (Basel III). http://www.bis.org/bcbs/basel3.htm

Borio C, Lowe P (2002) Assessing the risk of banking crises. BIS Q Rev Dec 43–54

Borio C, Lowe P (2004) Securing sustainable price stability: should credit come back from the wilderness? BIS working papers 157

Calomiris C (1999) Building an incentive-compatible safety net. J Bank Finance 23(10):1499–1519

Chamon M, Crowe C (2012) 'Predictive' indicators of crises. In: Caprio G (ed) Handbook in financial globalization: the evidence and impact of financial globalization. Elsevier, London, pp 499–505

Edge R, Meisenzahl R (2011) The unreliability of credit-to-GDP ratio gaps in real-time: implications for countercyclical capital buffers. Int J Central Banking 7(4):261–298

Goldstein I (2010) Fundamentals or panic: lessons from the empirical literature on financial crises. Encyclopedia of financial globalization

Hahm JH, Shin HS, Shin K (2013) Monetary aggregates and the procyclicality of the financial system: an Asian perspective. Working paper presented at ADB interim conference, Hong Kong, China, Jan 2013

Hattori M, Shin HS, Takahashi W (2009) A financial system perspective on Japan's experience in the late 1980s. Bank of Japan IMES discussion paper presented at the 16th Bank of Japan international conference, Tokyo, May 2009

Himmelberg C, Mayer C, Sinai T (2005) Assessing high house prices: bubbles, fundamentals, and misperceptions. NBER working paper 11643

Ivashina V, Scharfstein D (2010) Bank lending during the financial crisis of 2008. J Financ Econ 97(3):319–338

Kaminsky G, Lizondo S, Reinhart C (1998) Leading indicators of currency crisis. IMF Staff Pap 45(1):1–48

Morris S, Shin HS (1998) Unique equilibrium in a model of self-fulfilling currency attacks. Am Econ Rev 88:587–597

Morris S, Shin HS (2001) Rethinking multiple equilibria in macroeconomic modelling. NBER Macroecon Annu 2000:139–161

Morris S, Shin HS (2008) Financial regulation in a system context. Brookings papers on economic activity, pp 229–274

Repullo R, Saurina J (2011) The countercyclical capital buffer of Basel III: a critical assessment. In: Dewatripont M, Freixas X (eds) The crisis aftermath: new regulatory paradigms. Centre for Economic Policy Research, London

Shin HS (2009) Reflections on northern rock: the bank run that heralded the global financial crisis. J Econ Perspect 23(1):101–119

Shin HS (2013) Procyclicality and the search for early warning indicators. IMF working papers 13/258

Shin HS, Shin K (2010) Procyclicality and monetary aggregates. NBER working paper W16836

Summers LH (1985) On economics and finance. J Finan 40(3):633–635

Chapter 4
Emerging Asia's Noncore Liabilities and Policy Effectiveness

Excess savings and rising capital inflows—especially since the early 2000s—gave Asia ample liquidity with lower borrowing costs. This would spur domestic demand and growth, helping begin the process of rebalancing the region's economic structure. As this happened, the behavior of economic agents—banks, firms, and households—also changed. The preference toward investing in financial assets increased. This added the risks of procyclicality discussed in previous chapters. Based on flow-of-fund analysis, we showed in Chap. 2 that the rise in bank assets in emerging Asia was driven by a surge in noncore liabilities associated with capital inflows. While this raised some concerns over its impact on financial stability, the precise extent and nature of the effect remains to be investigated. To what extent does the rise in noncore bank liabilities threaten Asia's financial stability, and how does it influence the effectiveness of standard monetary policy?

Compared with other emerging markets, Asia's noncore liabilities as a share of total liabilities remain relatively small. But their rapid rise and higher ratio to gross domestic product (GDP) may have reduced the effectiveness of monetary policy. When the policy is overstressed by continuing to raise the interest rates with limited effect on noncore liabilities, we show in this chapter that it can produce unintended side effects such as elevating probabilities of bankruptcy. Hence, making financial stability an additional goal would require an additional policy instrument. As done in the previous chapters, here we continue to argue that an effective macroprudential policy is needed to supplement standard monetary policy.

After analyzing the relative size of noncore bank liabilities, we analyze the emerging comovement between bank credit and noncore liabilities. This is done using a credit model that takes into account the financial structure of lenders and borrowers (credit channel hypothesis). We then test the effectiveness of interest rate policy, followed by its impact on the probability of bankruptcies occurring.

Coauthored with Marthe Hinojales.

I.J. Azis and H.S. Shin, *Managing Elevated Risk*,
DOI 10.1007/978-981-287-284-5_4

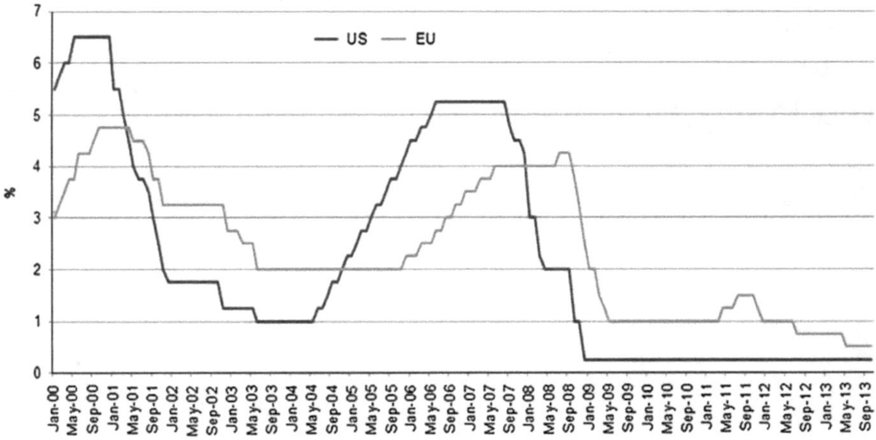

Fig. 4.1 Interest rates—United States (US), Europe. *Source* European Central Bank and US Federal Reserve

4.1 Bank-Led Flows, Noncore Liabilities, and Credit Growth

While push and pull factors work to fuel capital flows, those since early 2000 were driven more by the push factor. United States (US) and Eurozone interest rates fluctuated sharply during the 2000s. After falling precipitously in 2001–2003 in response to the 2000 recession and the 11 September 2001 political shock, the US Federal Funds rate began to rise, increasing more than fivefold by the end of 2007. But the global financial crisis of 2008/2009 dramatically reversed the trend, pushing rates down to as low as 0.25 %. The European interest rates essentially followed the pattern (Fig. 4.1).

Global liquidity conditions have changed since (Fig. 4.2). Massive amounts of capital shifted from advanced economies to emerging markets.[1] Emerging Europe and Asia were among the biggest recipients. This is the first phase of global liquidity. Much of these inflows were intermediated through banks (bank-led flows). As these should appear as bank liabilities, any volatility would likely have ramifications for bank balance sheets—implying the risk of procyclicality. During the 2008/2009 global financial crisis, these flows were briefly interrupted. But after mid-2010, large flows returned. This time they were predominantly channeled through capital

[1] Mckinnon (2012) argued that the easy money policy in advanced economies provokes global monetary instability through capital flows led by "carry traders" who exploit interest rate differentials across countries. He further noted the policy was also less effective than originally thought in generating recovery (e.g., in the US). Azis (2010) also argued that a premature US recovery would unlikely be sustainable. Rather than forcing a quick recovery, structural changes in the US financial system were needed more.

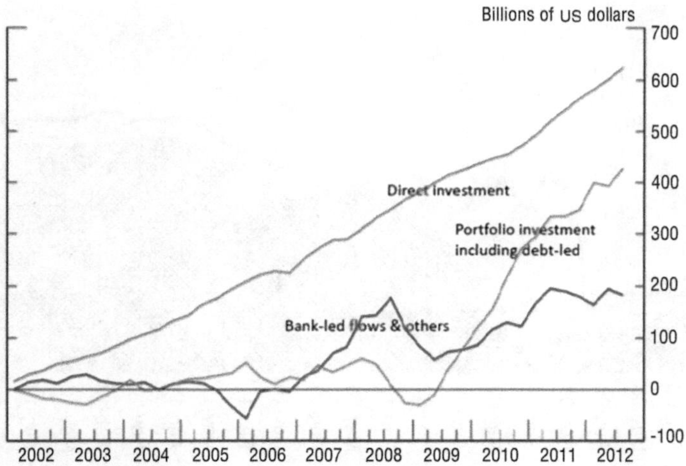

Fig. 4.2 Gross capital flows by type—emerging markets. *Source* Institute of International Finance

markets (debt-led flows), including local currency (LCY) bond markets. The push came from the elevated risk and falling yields in the US following the unprecedented quantitative easing (QE) by the US Federal Reserve (US Fed). QE essentially involves large-scale asset purchase to halt the precipitous fall in asset prices. After adjusted twice, by late December 2012, monthly purchases reached $85 billion (Fig. 4.3). Thus, the second phase of global liquidity began. The nature and protagonist of capital flows changed and so did the impending risks.[2]

How significant is the link between bank-led flows and noncore liabilities? Figure 4.4 summarizes this link for emerging Asia. As the cumulative change (increase) of bank-led flows surged before the global financial crisis, so did noncore bank liabilities. When they dropped off during the crisis, the cumulative change of noncore liabilities also declined, before surging back from 2009 to 2012.[3] The US Fed announcement over the possibility of policy normalization and QE tapering in mid-2013 rattled several emerging Asian markets. Together with the growing expectation that recovery in advanced economies was imminent, it led to capital outflows and another round of volatility. As shown in Fig. 4.4, bank-led flows fell during 2012–2014, causing noncore liabilities to fall as well. Clearly,

[2] As discussed in Chap. 2, debt-led flows and bank-led flows have been the most volatile among all types of capital flows.

[3] We argued in Chap. 3 that the exact dividing line between core and noncore liabilities highly depends on the financial system in question, its degree of openness, and financial market and institutional development. Retail household deposits would be a good first conjecture in defining core liabilities. Given data limitations, however, here we define noncore liabilities based on the claim holder, or meaning the total liabilities less retail/household deposits.

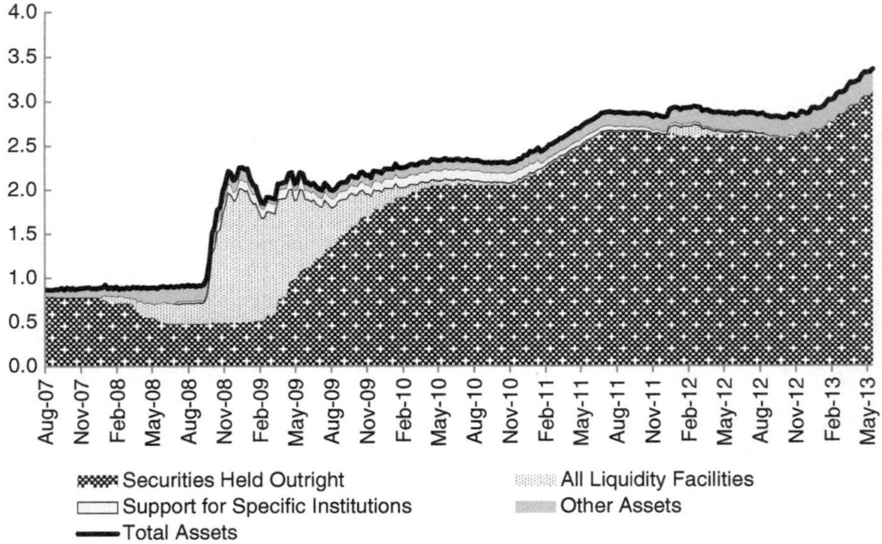

Fig. 4.3 Quantitative easing—United States Federal Reserve Assets Outstanding ($ trillion). *Source* US Federal Reserve

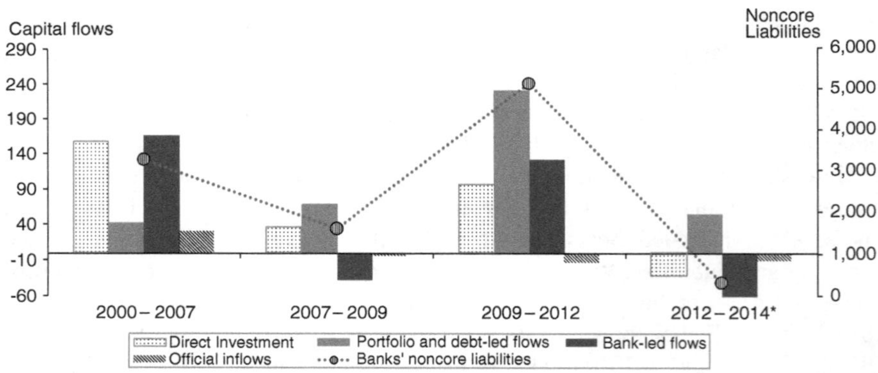

Fig. 4.4 Capital inflows and noncore liabilities—emerging Asia (cumulative change, $ billion). *Asterisk* (*) figures are IIF estimate (2013) and IIF forecast (2014). *Notes* Emerging Asia refers to China, People's Republic of; India; Indonesia; the Republic of Korea; Malaysia; the Philippines; and Thailand. Noncore liabilities data do not include India and the Philippines. **Bank-led flows** = Net disbursements from commercial banks (excluding credits guaranteed or insured under credit programs of creditor governments). This generally includes bond purchases by commercial banks. **Portfolio and debt-led flows** = Equity investment and net external financing provided by all other private creditors. The latter includes flows from nonbank sources into bond markets, as well as deposits in local banks by nonresidents other than banks. It also includes credit by suppliers (excluding credits guaranteed or insured under credit program of creditor governments), identified private placements of debt securities, and other financial securities issued in local or foreign currencies. Finally, it includes estimated interest payments due but not paid and estimated payments flows with private creditors other than commercial banks resulting from discounted debt transactions. *Source* IIF and national sources

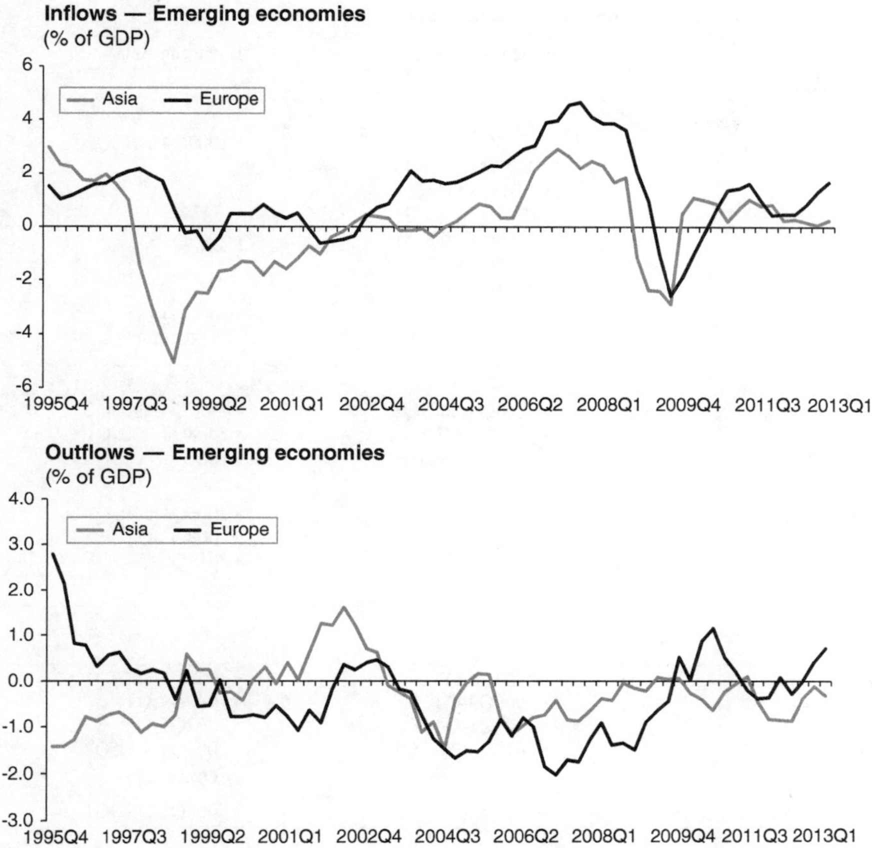

Fig. 4.5 Bank flows to emerging economies (% of GDP). *Notes* Asia includes Indonesia, the Republic of Korea, the Philippines, and Thailand. Europe includes Bulgaria, Croatia, Czech Republic, Hungary, Latvia, Poland, Russia, Turkey, and Ukraine. *Source* ADB calculations using data from CEIC

bank-led flows have been the major driver behind the increase in noncore liabilities during that period (see Appendix for the impact on individual economies).[4]

To gain a better perspective on the size of bank-led flows, we compare the case of emerging Asia with that of emerging Europe (Fig. 4.5).[5] Prior to the 1997/1998

[4] Note that Fig. 4.4 also confirms the different phases of capital flows in emerging Asia, where bank-led flows dominate phase 1 and portfolio and debt-led flows dominate phase 2.

[5] Emerging Europe includes Bulgaria; Croatia; Czech Republic; Hungary; Latvia; Poland; the Russian Federation; Turkey; and Ukraine.

Table 4.1 Episodes of capital flows—selected emerging economies

Led by	Emerging Europe	Emerging Asia
Gross inflows		
Surge		
Bank flows	• 2005Q2-Q3 • 2006Q4-2007Q3 • 2010Q3-Q4 • 2012Q4-2013Q1	• 2009Q4-2010Q2
Debt flows	• 1997Q3-1998Q1 • 2002Q3-Q4 • 2004Q2-Q4	• 2002Q1-Q3
Equity flows	–	• 1999Q2-Q3
FDI flows	–	–
Stop		
Bank flows	• 2008Q4-2009Q3 • 2012Q1-Q2	• 1997Q4-1998Q2 • 2008Q4-2009Q1
Debt flows	• 1998Q4-1999Q2	• 1997Q1-Q3 • 2001Q1-Q3
Equity flows	–	• 2006Q4-2007Q1 • 2008Q1-Q3 • 2011Q3-Q4
FDI flows	–	–
Gross outflows		
Retrenchment		
Bank flows	• 2002Q1-Q2 • 2005Q3-Q4 • 2009Q1-Q4 • 2012Q3-2013Q1	• 1996Q4-1997Q1 • 1998Q3-Q4 • 2002Q1-Q2 • 2004Q4-2005Q2
Debt flows	–	• 1998Q1-Q2
Equity flows	–	• 2008Q2-2009Q1
FDI flows	–	–
Flight		
Bank flows	• 1996Q3-Q4 • 2004Q1-Q2 • 2011Q2-Q3	• 2002Q4-2003Q2 • 2006Q1-Q2
Debt flows	–	• 2009Q4-2010Q2
Equity flows	–	• 2007Q2-Q4
FDI flows	• 2003Q2-Q4 • 2007Q1-Q3	–

FDI foreign direct investment

Notes

1. Emerging Europe refers to Bulgaria, Croatia, Czech Republic, Hungary, Latvia, Poland, Russia, Turkey, and Ukraine. Emerging Asia refers to Indonesia, the Republic of Korea, the Philippines, and Thailand
2. Episodes are based on 1 standard deviation (SD) band of gross capital inflows and outflows
3. Surge episode = if the year-on-year level change of gross inflows (based on a 4-quarter moving sum) increases more than 1 SD above its rolling 8-quarter mean. Stop = if the year-on-year level change of gross inflows (based on a 4-quarter moving sum) falls 1 SD below its rolling 8-quarter mean. Retrenchment = year-on-year level change of gross outflows (based on a 4-quarter moving sum) increases more than 1 SD above its rolling 8-quarter mean. Flight = if the year-on-year level change of gross outflows (based on a 4-quarter moving sum) falls 1 SD below its rolling 8-quarter mean

Source Authors' calculations

Asian financial crisis, the size of bank-led inflows as a percentage of GDP was larger in Asia than in Europe. Afterward—until 2002—flows in emerging Europe fluctuated only slightly, while those in Asia fell precipitously. Until a few years prior to the global financial crisis, emerging Europe's share was persistently higher than Asia's. The trend in bank-led outflows was generally similar. But the peak in both regions occurred at about the same time, just before the global financial crisis—coinciding with the fall in interest rates in the US and Europe.

As in Asia, volatility in emerging Europe has been also highest for bank-led and debt-led flows (Table 4.1). A closer look reveals that the occurrence of "surge" of both types of flows occurred more frequently in emerging Europe than in emerging Asia.

To the extent both emerging Europe and Asia are highly bank dependent, significant volatility in noncore liabilities could pose a serious procyclicality risk. This would not happen, however, if the size of noncore liabilities is small, and more importantly, if bank assets are not deeply affected by the growth and relative change in noncore liabilities. To determine size, we first compare noncore liabilities in Asia with those in emerging Europe. Noncore liabilities in Asia—measured as percentage to GDP—have been on an upward trend since the Asian financial crisis (Fig. 4.6). But they are smaller than in emerging Europe. Much of the reason is because there was a jump in noncore liabilities in Europe driven by increased bank-led flows as discussed in Chap. 2. Broken down by economy, by 2012, only Hong Kong, China; Singapore; and the Republic of Korea had a higher share of noncore liabilities than most of emerging Europe (Fig. 4.7). However, measured by the ratio of noncore liabilities to total liabilities, Asia's share of noncore liabilities is relatively high (Fig. 4.8). It ranged from around 40 % (in Indonesia) to over 50 % (in the Republic of Korea).

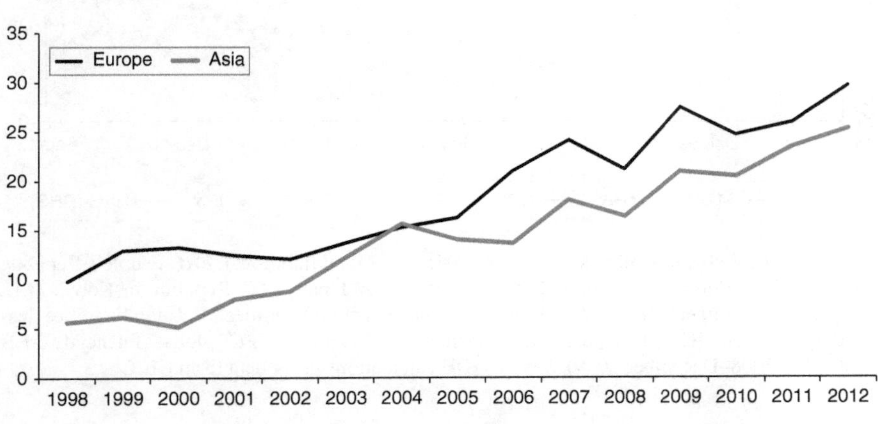

Fig. 4.6 Noncore bank liabilities—emerging economies (% of gross domestic product). *Notes* Asia includes People's Republic of China; Hong Kong, China; Indonesia; Malaysia; the Philippines; the Republic of Korea; Singapore; Taipei,China; and Thailand. Europe includes Bulgaria, Croatia, Czech Republic, Hungary, Latvia, Poland, Russia, Turkey, and Ukraine. *Source* ADB calculations using data from CEIC

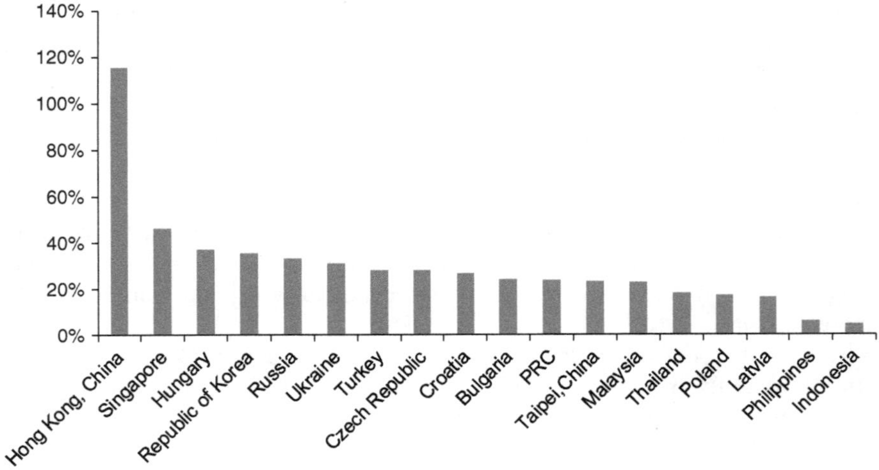

Fig. 4.7 Noncore bank liabilities—selected emerging economies (% of gross domestic product, 2012). *PRC* People's Republic of China. *Source* ADB calculations using data from Bankscope

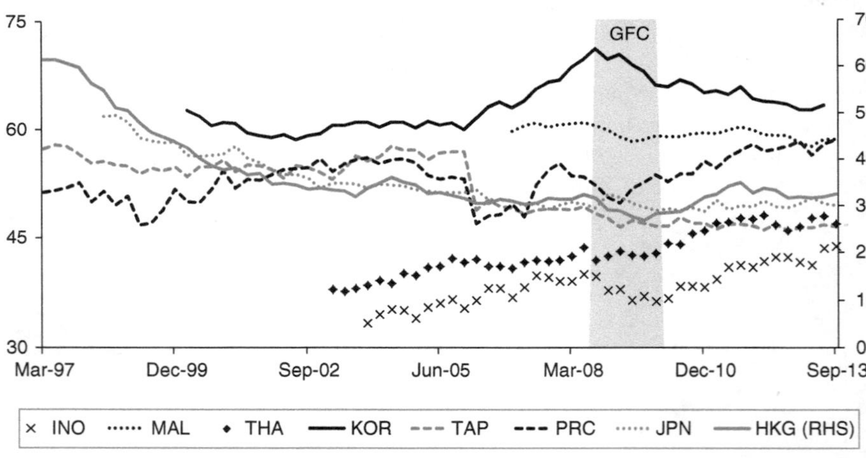

Fig. 4.8 Noncore bank liabilities—emerging Asia (% of total liabilities). *PRC* People's Republic of China; *HKG* Hong Kong, China; *INO* Indonesia; *JPN* Japan; *KOR* Republic of Korea; *MAL* Malaysia; *TAP* Taipei,China; *THA* Thailand. *Note* Noncore liabilities = Total liabilities less retail/household/individual deposits and shareholders' equity. *GFC* global financial crisis (September 2008–December 2009). *Source* ADB calculations using data from CEIC

To examine whether increases in noncore liabilities mirror increases in total assets, we plot the changes in bank assets against changes in noncore and core liabilities (Fig. 4.9). The slope of noncore liabilities is higher than that of core liabilities in all economies. This is consistent with the analysis based on the

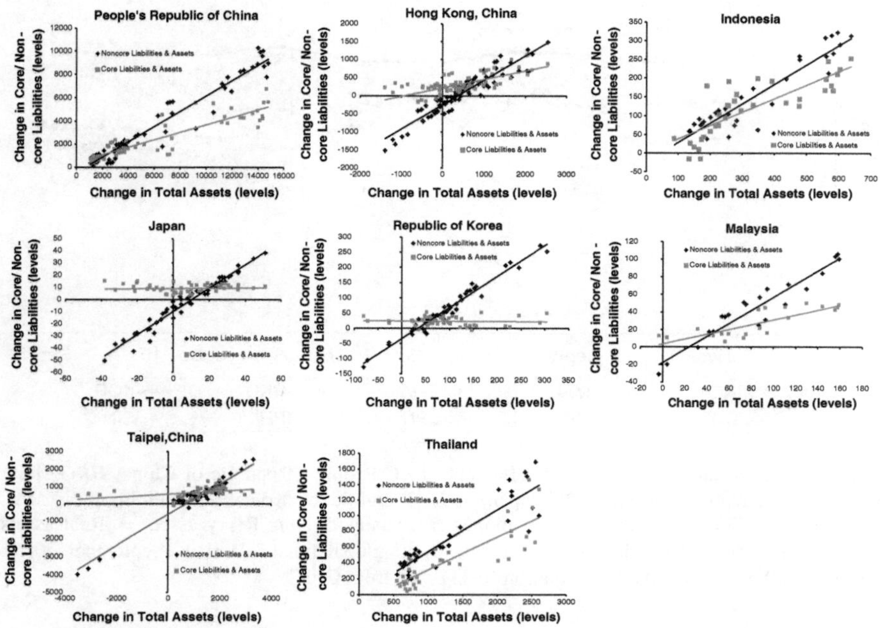

Fig. 4.9 Changes in core and noncore liabilities versus changes in total assets (year-on-year change in quarterly levels). *Source* Authors' calculations

Flow-of-Fund data in Chap. 2, although here we use the information directly obtained from the banking sector with greater detail and more complete data. It suggests that the growth in bank assets move more closely with changes in noncore liabilities than with changes in core liabilities, confirming the former's increasing importance in bank decisions to expand. Based on the current size of noncore liabilities, however, the risk of procyclicality in emerging Asia is not yet large. However, given their rising trend and high ratio to total liabilities, policy-makers and regulators should monitor developments closely. If left unattended, they could reach a level that could threaten macroeconomic and financial stability.

How did banks allocate spending and investment given their rise in assets? It has been shown that bank preference toward investing in risky financial assets increased along with the increase in noncore liabilities (Azis and Yarcia 2014). Holding financial assets such as bonds and other securities remain high on bank balance sheets. At least 50 % of total bank assets are classified as risky. As depicted in Fig. 4.10, the increase in risky assets as a percentage of total assets after the global financial crisis is noticeable in some economies (Indonesia, Malaysia, and Thailand). Yet, bank credits remain dominant (Fig. 4.11). In emerging Asia (except Singapore), loans or bank credits hold the largest share of bank assets. And they are all rising, albeit at different speeds.

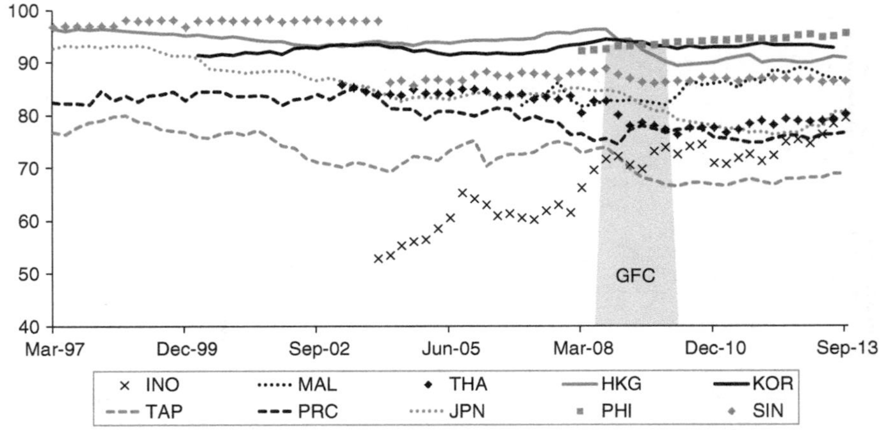

Fig. 4.10 Risky bank assets (% of total assets). *PRC* People's Republic of China; *HKG* Hong Kong, China; *INO* Indonesia; *JPN* Japan; *KOR* Republic of Korea; *PHI* Philippines; *MAL* Malaysia; *SIN* Singapore; *TAP* Taipei,China; *THA* Thailand. *Note* Risky assets = Total assets less cash, government bonds and fixed assets. *GFC* global financial crisis (September 2008–December 2009). *Source* ADB calculations using data from CEIC

But two variables moving in the same direction (credits and noncore liabilities) do not necessarily imply causality. To explore further, we construct a credit regression model with the usual control variables (Table 4.2). In Model-1, the growth of the economy, interest rates and bank net worth (to capture banks financial health) all determine credit growth. The coefficients are all significant. Controlling for these variables, changes in noncore liabilities turn out to be the most significant over the period. To the extent government bonds in these economies have been growing steadily and provide an alternative source of long-term financing, we include changes in bond yields in Model-3. The notion that earnings from higher bond yields may "crowd out" credit is tested. While the added variable has the expected sign, however, it is insignificant. More importantly, changes in noncore liabilities remain the most significant variable.

In modeling credit growth, it has been also hypothesized that credit growth is not only determined by the size of a bank's available funds, but also by changes in net worth and external finance premiums of both borrowers and lenders. This "credit channel" hypothesis was first postulated by Bernanke et al. (1996) and elaborated further in Stiglitz and Greenwald (2003), Stiglitz (2001), among others.

Why does a borrower's balance sheet matter? When firms act as lenders to other firms, credit market friction will likely amplify, propagating real and nominal shocks to the economy (Stiglitz and Greenwald 2003). In a principal–agent problem, credit and investment cycles can be affected in several ways. A depressed collateral value of the firm due to falling asset prices, or a worsening balance sheet caused by a double mismatch in the firm's leverage, can raise the agency costs

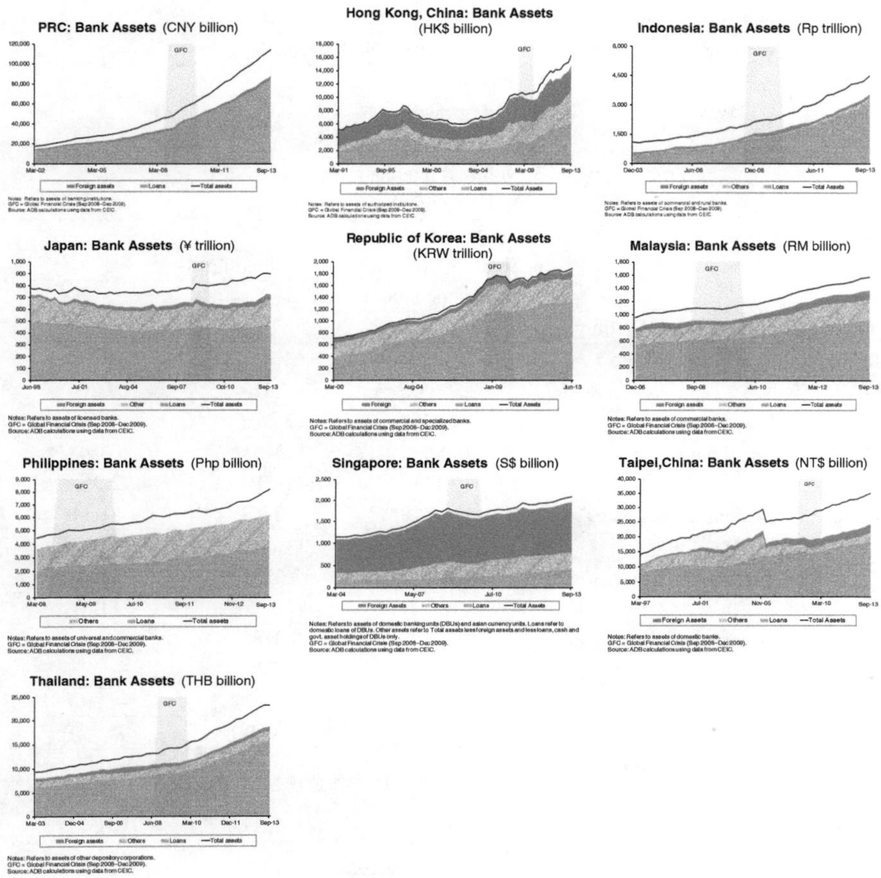

Fig. 4.11 Trends in bank assets—selected Asian economies

imposed by asymmetric information between borrowers and lenders.[6] In these circumstances, there is an incentive for borrowers to pass off risky or potentially bad projects as good projects to lenders. This can lower the probability that the loan will be repaid, or raise the probability that the firm will go bankrupt. While the causality between interest rates and bankruptcies can work both ways, it will nonetheless lead to higher costs of external finance (e.g., in higher interest rates).[7]

[6] Stiglitz and Weiss (1981) demonstrate the effect of lenders' inability to distinguish between different types of borrowers on credit restrictions through the agency cost. Williamson (1987) shows that even if lenders know the risk characteristics of different borrowers, there is an incentive for lenders to verify borrower claims and monitor the project, raising costs that can lead to credit rationing.

[7] The cost difference between external finance and internally generated finance is a measure of agency cost, which likely increases during recessions and decreases during booms.

Table 4.2 Regression results on credit growth

Dependent variable	Independent variable (expected sign)
Credit growth	Change in:
	1. GDP growth (+)
	2. Bank net worth (+)
	3. Nominal interest rates (−)
	4. Noncore liabilities (+)
	5. Corporate net worth (+)
	6. Share of government bond holdings (−)
	7. Government bond yields (−)

Panel regression results (Credit growth = Y)

Independent variables	Model-1	Model-2	Model-3
GDP growth	0.065**	0.0826**	0.026
	(1.97)	(2.26)	(0.84)
Change in banks' net worth$_{t-1}$	0.042**	0.049**	0.054***
	(2.15)	(2.24)	(2.95)
Change in nominal interest rates$_{t-1}$	−0.728***	−0.976***	−1.348***
	(−2.62)	(−3.12)	(−4.10)
Change in noncore liabilities$_{t-1}$	0.536***	0.635***	0.384***
	(18.74)	(20.65)	(11.3)
Change in corporate net worth$_{t-1}$	–	0.018	–
	–	(0.72)	–
Change in share of government bond holdings$_{t-1}$	–	−0.008	–
	–	(−0.48)	–
Change in government bond yields	–	–	−0.002
	–	–	(−0.39)
Constant	0.042***	0.029***	0.062***
	(5.42)	(7.32)	(9.09)
R-squared			
Within	0.484	0.484	0.294
Between	0.897	0.901	0.920
Overall	0.613	0.613	0.551

GDP = gross domestic product
Note z-values in parenthesis
***Significant at 1 %
**Significant at 5 %
*Significant at 10 %
Source Authors' calculations

Why does the financial structure of lenders matter? If a bank holds large amounts of nonliquid assets (government bonds) and a considerable number of nonperforming loans (higher defaults), then the collateral of financial intermediaries will likely fall. This forces lenders to undertake portfolio reallocations that may result in credit rationing. In this situation, at any given interest rate, fewer funds or credits are available.

Following this hypothesis, in Model-2, we include the net worth of borrowers represented by corporates and changes in the share of bondholdings in total bank assets. The latter is included for two reasons: First, to reduce risks, banks tend to accumulate government bonds to comply with the capital adequacy ratio (CAR) rule; and second, the rising share of government bonds may limit a bank's capacity to lend. As shown in Table 4.2, the two variables have the expected signs, but none are significant. More importantly, the coefficient of noncore liabilities is even higher than in Model-1 and Model-3 (0.635), and it has a higher degree of significance as well. So the result showing that noncore liabilities contribute significantly to bank credit growth is robust.

Expanding bank credit itself can be positive if it is in line with the bank's capacity to lend—based on stable sources and real demand. The problem is more often than not that credit growth tends to be excessive as liquidity becomes abundant, creating a lending boom that could threaten financial stability. Although we argued in Chap. 3 that credit size may not be the best early warning indicator, how credit is allocated remains important as a measure of vulnerability. If a considerable portion of credit goes to nonproductive sectors, the growth of monetary aggregates will not be in sync with what the economy is able to create. Low productivity and high inflation will likely follow this kind of credit growth. Moreover, a surge of bank lending to housing and real estate can also contribute to asset bubbles and propagating financial instability. Data show most emerging Asian economies are experiencing this trend. Measured as a percentage of GDP, housing and real estate loans have been on the rise, with the highest ratio since the onset of the global financial crisis in Singapore and Hong Kong, China (Fig. 4.12).

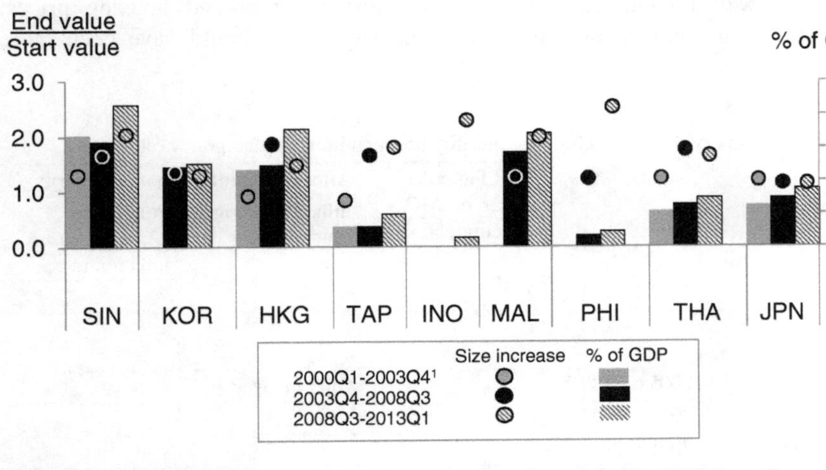

Fig. 4.12 Housing and real estate loans (size increase and % of GDP). *HKG* Hong Kong, China; *INO* Indonesia; *JPN* Japan; *KOR* Republic of Korea; *PHI* Philippines; *MAL* Malaysia; *SIN* Singapore; *TAP* Taipei,China; *THA* Thailand. *GDP* gross domestic product. Note Uses quarterly data. Data unavailable for PRC. Start of data except for INO (2010Q3); JPN (2000Q4); KOR (2005Q4); MAL (2006Q1); and PHI (2008Q2). *Source* ADB calculations using data from CEIC

4.2 Reassessing Monetary Policy

If the growth of noncore liabilities is the reason behind excessive credit expansion, the standard monetary policy of limiting credit growth can be ineffective. A better policy should then entail supervising and managing noncore liabilities. In Chap. 2, we explain that rising noncore liabilities associated with bank-led flows could be highly procyclical and constitute an important transmission channel of global liquidity shocks to emerging Asia. A likely outcome is that financial cycles will fall out of sync with domestic business cycles, meaning the effectiveness of a standard monetary policy can be severely curtailed. Similarly, when portfolio and debt-led flows became dominant (the second phase), nonbank activities can influence monetary aggregates, in which case, a standard monetary policy also tends to be ineffective. The increased preference of economic agents toward risky assets further complicates the policy challenge. It is on this ground we argue that a supplementary macroprudential policy is needed.

In an environment where monetary policy is effective, credit growth that fuels inflation can be controlled by interest rates. With varying degree of success, this has been the approach widely used by monetary authorities. The reality, however, does not seem to support the intended purpose. Our simple test on the effectiveness of interest rate policy to lower the inflation rate in emerging Asia shows a mixed result at best (Table 4.3). The test summary shows that it is the inflation rate that Granger causes the policy rate, not the other way around. This is particularly true in the People's Republic of China; Hong Kong, China; Indonesia; the Republic of Korea; the Philippines; and Viet Nam. And we do not find a significant relationship between the two variables in India, Malaysia, or Thailand.

The limited capacity of monetary policy to prevent an economy from overheating is well known, especially when involving asset and housing prices. But controlling credit growth through monetary policy should have been more

Table 4.3 Summary results on Granger causality between inflation and policy rate

	Sample	VAR lag order (based on AIC selection)	After correcting for nonstationarity	
			Inflation Granger causes policy rate	Policy rate Granger causes inflation rate
PRC	2001.1–2011.7	2	/	/
Hong Kong, China	2001.1–2011.7	1	/	x
Indonesia	2005.6–2011.7	2	Only in lag 1	x
India	2001.1–2011.7	2	x	x
Korea, Rep. of	2001.1–2011.7	2	/	x
Malaysia	2004.4–2011.7	1	x	x
Philippines	2001.1–2011.7	3	/	x
Thailand	2007.7–2011.7	1	x	x
Viet Nam	2001.1–2011.7	2	/	x

straightforward had the financing source for credit been known and influenced by interest rates—bank deposits, for example. Yet, the share of nondeposit and other noncore liabilities to finance credit has been growing, making it more difficult to control. This may explain the ineffectiveness of interest rate policy in containing credit growth and hence inflation. A set of institutional factors may have influenced the transmission of interest rates to inflation rates.

Returning our focus to the effect of monetary policy on noncore liabilities, we run a model that directly relates interest rates with noncore liabilities. Our intention is not to capture the causal relationship of the two variables. Instead, we want to determine how bank liabilities respond to interest rates (proxied by discount or policy rates) in 10 Asian economies. For the reasons described in Chap. 2, different financial institutions may have different capacities of what they can easily absorb on their balance sheets in terms of capital inflows. With a wider global network, foreign banks may have greater access to external financing compared with domestic banks. Furthermore, there may be differences in domestic and foreign bank behavior—as evident in the trend of their noncore liability holdings over the years. Thus, the specified model below is separately applied to domestic banks and foreign banks for 1998–2012.

Ln(noncore liabilities) = Ln(GDP) + policy rate, *where the policy rate variables include the current and the lag.*

If monetary policy is effective, the coefficients of the interest rate variables would be significant and have a negative sign. After controlling for GDP growth, none of the policy rate coefficients—when ran against noncore liabilities—are found significant (Table 4.4). While the GDP coefficients in all cases are significant (and

Table 4.4 Regression results on policy rates and bank liabilities

	Dependent variable			
	Noncore liabilities	Core liabilities	Noncore liabilities	Core liabilities
Independent variables	Domestic banks		Foreign banks	
Ln.GDP growth	0.736***	0.944**	0.446*	0.347**
	(3.05)	(3.77)	(2.14)	(1.87)
Policy rate$_{t-1}$	−0.050	−0.068	−0.058	−0.068
	(−0.64)	(−0.98)	(−0.83)	(−1.12)
Policy rate$_t$	−0.185	−0.268**	−0.085	−0.077
	(−1.40)	(−2.24)	(−0.66)	(−0.69)
Constant	10.289***	10.502***	11.177***	14.087***
	(4.23)	(4.14)	(5.38)	−7.620

Note z-values in parenthesis
***Significant at 1 %
**Significant at 5 %
*Significant at 10 %
Source Authors' calculations

with the correct sign), the policy rates with and without lag—although negative—are not. Additionally, the policy rate coefficients for foreign banks' noncore liabilities are almost zero.

To the extent the effect of monetary policy is more instantaneous than most other aggregate demand policies, the current policy rate (without lag) may be more appropriate to evaluate. Interestingly, in using this rate, the only policy rate coefficient that is significant and with the correct sign is for domestic banks' core liabilities (at the 5 % level). For the rest, the coefficient is either insignificant or very small. The results thereby confirm the limited effectiveness of standard monetary policy in containing the growth of noncore liabilities.

However, the explanations and fundamental reasons for policy ineffectiveness could be easily overlooked. After policy is implemented and the intended goal is not met—whether targeted inflation, the size of noncore liabilities, or credit growth—there is a tendency to even double efforts by tightening monetary policy further. Not only will the goal continue to be unmet—precisely because of the reasons described above—but there is also a risk that the financial health of banks deteriorates due to too tightened monetary conditions. We can look at this issue further by focusing on how policy rates affect bank wealth—the latter measured by the ratio of bank net worth to safe assets.

The following set of explanatory variables is specified. Growth of GDP represents the overall economic activity that should have a positive contribution to bank wealth. Next is bank profitability measured as the difference between lending and discount rates. Higher profitability should augment bank wealth too. Given the role of equity markets in asset valuation, especially the financial sector component of the stock market, a bank's financial condition is also influenced by fluctuations in that market. Improving stock indexes would help improve bank net worth. After controlling for these variables, we then test the role of policy rates in affecting bank wealth. Given a certain level of interest rate, an increase could help improve bank revenues and deposits, thereby augmenting net worth. But when bank loans start to suffer, a further interest rate increase will diminish bank wealth. To capture these dynamics, we include a squared policy rate in the model.

Table 4.5 shows the results. All explanatory variables are significant at least at the 5 % level and have the expected signs. What is interesting is that the coefficient for policy rate is positive and significant at the 1 % level, but for the squared rate, it is negative and also significant at 1 %. This suggests that up to a certain point, raising interest rates will have a positive impact on bank net worth. But continuing to raise rates beyond that point would damage a bank's financial health. If left untreated, the deterioration of net worth could lead to bankruptcy.

Table 4.5 Regression results on policy rates and bankruptcy

	Dependent variable
	Bankruptcy indicator[a]
Independent variables	Full sample
Lending–discount rate gap (e.g., profitability measure)	0.002**
	(2.15)
Change in financial stock index	0.126***
	(5.44)
Policy rate_t	0.118***
	(7.77)
Policy rate, squared	−0.007***
	(−4.82)
Change in real GDP	0.056**
	(1.64)
Constant	−0.889**
	(−2.82)
R-squared	
Within	0.2031
Between	0.1687
Overall	0.2458

[a]Calculated as net worth/nonrisky assets
Note z-values in parenthesis
***Significant at 1 %
**Significant at 5 %
*Significant at 10 %
Source Authors' calculations

As potent as monetary policy can be, the increasing role of noncore liabilities in influencing credit clearly points to the need for supplementary measures to make monetary policy more effective. This is where we strongly argue that policy needs to be complemented by macroprudential measures. Designed properly, these measures could also help reduce the risk of financial vulnerability caused by changes in global liquidity.

4.3 Appendix

See Fig. 4.13.

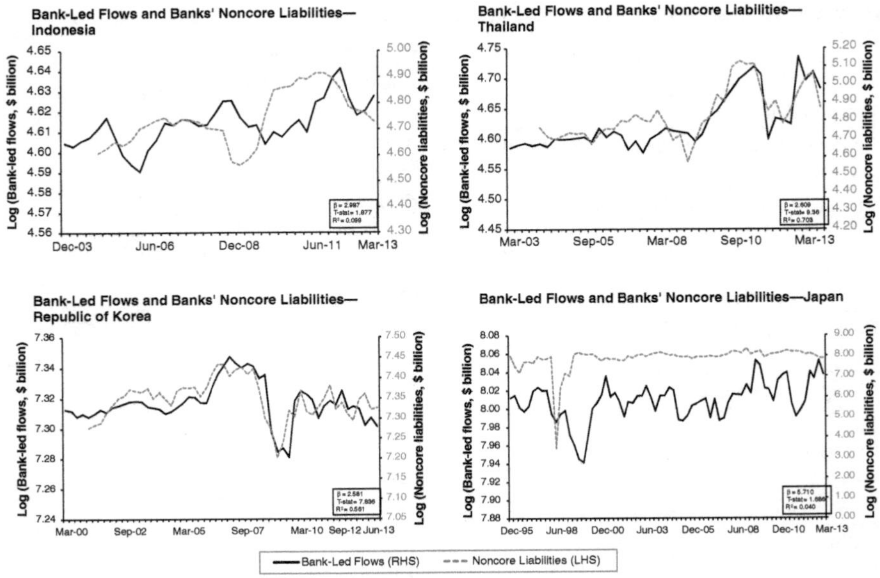

Fig. 4.13 Bank-led flows and noncore liabilities. *Notes* (1) Levels (in USD billion) are log-transformed. (2) Noncore liabilities = Total liabilities less retail/household/individual deposits and shareholders' equity. (3) Regression results are for log-transformed variables (where y = noncore liabilities; x = bank-led flows). *Source* ADB calculations using data from Balance of Payments Statistics, International Monetary Fund; and CEIC

References

Azis IJ (2010) Predicting a recovery date from the economic crisis of 2008. Socio-Econ Plann Sci 44:122–129

Azis IJ, Yarcia D (2014) How capital flows affect economy-wide vulnerability and inequality: flow-of-funds analysis of selected Asian economies. ADB working paper series on regional economic integration 136

Bernanke B, Gertler M, Gilchrist S (1996) The financial accelerator and the flight to quality. Rev Econ Stat 78(1):1–15

Mckinnon R (2012) Zero interest rates in the United States provoke world monetary instability and constrict the US economy. Stanford University SIEPR policy brief

Stiglitz J (2001) Information and the change in the paradigm in economics. Prize lecture, Nobel Foundation, Stockholm

Stiglitz J, Greenwald B (2003) Towards a new paradigm in monetary economics. Cambridge University Press, Cambridge

Stiglitz J, Weiss A (1981) Credit rationing in markets with imperfect information. Am Econ Rev 71(3):393–410

Williamson S (1987) Costly monitoring, loan contracts, and equilibrium credit rationing. Q J Econ 102(1):135–145

Chapter 5
Capital Flows and Income Distribution

The analysis so far has shown how global liquidity—boosted by easy money policy in advanced economies—has affected emerging markets, particularly in Asia. The focus has been on the implications on financial and macroeconomic stability and on the behavior of economic agents. It has also pointed to the limited effectiveness of standard monetary policy and the need for developing new early warning indicators. From the development perspective, it is also of interest to find out how changing global liquidity and capital flows may affect socioeconomic issues such as income inequality, unemployment, and poverty. In this chapter, we show in particular how capital inflows to emerging Asia can also change these indicators.

Using a general equilibrium framework with a financial module, we show the mechanism for how seemingly unrelated financial phenomena are in fact closely interlinked with income inequality, unemployment, and poverty. We argue that while helping boost economic growth, capital inflow surges can create not only financial instability, but also worsen conditions in terms of these socioeconomic indicators. More particularly, in the case of increased bank-led flows, the impact critically depends on whether or not recipient banks take on more risk. By combining model-based results applied to a particular case in one Asian economy—where massive capital inflows came in response to easy money and low interest rates in advanced economies, and where income disparity is rising—we show that when banks become more risky, the impact of increased bank-led flows on growth, macroeconomic aggregates, household income distribution, unemployment, and poverty are not favorable.

With these results, we then discuss measures that could help prevent banks from taking on excessive risk. Using a theory-based ranking and by considering the benefits, opportunities, costs, and risks of alternative criteria and policies, we find that imposing a macroprudential levy on bank-led flows, the same tool we proposed in a previous chapter, can indeed produce more favorable results. Furthermore, taking into account several criteria and factors, we argue that this policy works not only for macroeconomic and micro-cum-financial stability, but

I.J. Azis and H.S. Shin, *Managing Elevated Risk*,
DOI 10.1007/978-981-287-284-5_5

also for socioeconomic objective. This reinforces the argument why a "second best" approach to liberalization is better than the "first best" approach. Despite the need for cooperation and policy coordination among countries, national policy should remain key when it comes to maintaining macrofinancial stability and improving socioeconomic conditions.

5.1 National Policy Remains Key

Although capital flows derive from push and pull factors—and hence should be ideally handled through policy cooperation and coordination among economies—in reality, policy makers in individual economies are forced to take unilateral policies. In most cases, regional and international policy coordination works only in theory. Indeed, even as economies become more interdependent, national policies continue to rule irrespective of spillovers to other economies and the talk of policy coordination and cooperation. The ultraeasy money policy in advanced economies discussed in Chaps. 2 and 4 is a recent example of this "financial nationalism." It had significant repercussions on global liquidity by generating massive capital flows. Despite the risks and potential damage capital flows can cause to other economies, no one can stop them—especially when the spread of returns (interest rates) is large and the growth differential between advanced and emerging markets is substantial. In effect, emerging markets at the receiving end ought to deal with the risks through unilateral national policies.

If capital inflows cause instability and eventually lead to a crisis, more often than not the socioeconomic repercussions are disastrous. In dealing with this, no global or regional policy initiative can substitute for good national policies. Indeed, the evidence where a standard policy response damages welfare is widespread—especially when governments are belt-tightening. For example, on 17 May 2012, a joint statement by the Director General of the International Labour Organization (ILO) and Secretary General of the Organisation for Economic Co-operation and Development (OECD) said that some 20 million jobs in both developed and developing economies had disappeared since the onset of the 2008/2009 global financial crisis, and 21 million jobs must be generated in G20 economies just to match the precrisis employment rate—impossible to achieve in the near term. If anything, the risk is the unemployment rate could increase. A crippled crisis-affected financial sector is bad enough; but nothing is worse than if the true costs are in terms of employment and the welfare of most people.[1]

The national policy most relevant to the phenomenon of capital flows is financial sector liberalization, where capital openness is a central component. Financial liberalization has been widely promoted as a way to better allocate capital and widen opportunities for savers and investors. It creates an environment

[1] For example, the environmental impact of a contagion-driven crisis poses another serious welfare risk. While a crisis can reduce pollution and resource consumption through reduced economic activity, a weakened economy also tends to lower environmental priorities.

conducive to financial innovation. Some argue that it also helps build discipline among policy makers in securing macroeconomic stability. This has been the predominant thinking for several decades.

One of the most important components—if controversial—of financial sector liberalization is capital account liberalization. Capital flows resulting from capital account liberalization are channeled through domestic intermediaries—either banks or firms—allowing greater competition and thus more efficiency. Countries freeing up their capital accounts often see a sudden jump in economic growth as they move away from financial repression. Yet, many of them, developing and developed economies alike, subsequently face instability, with some eventually suffering financial crisis.[2]

When confronted with this, defenders of capital account liberalization often cite the lack of preconditions before liberalizing to explain why crises emerge. They blame institutional factors like corruption, weak enforcement, and limited understanding on how a liberalized financial sector operates. Policy recommendations thus center on fixing those institutional factors; they never question the virtue of capital account liberalization itself. But the shocks that hit the US beginning in 2007 and the later Eurozone crisis are counterevidence that this is based on an erroneous hypothesis. The institutional quality in the US and Europe are supposedly better than most emerging market economies, yet they could not escape from crisis.

Only recently have analysts and scholars admitted that early preaching on financial sector liberalization and capital account liberalization was flawed (CIEPR 2012). They now admit that the "first best" approach of financial liberalization—where frictionless outcomes are emphasized—is faulty and should be replaced by a "second best" approach in which financial regulation is given far greater importance, and where capital controls are no longer taboo. After decades of preaching the virtues of cross-border capital flows, the International Monetary Fund (IMF) finally admitted that some restrictions on capital flows can help protect an economy from financial turmoil. Central to the analysis is the need to maintain financial stability and macroprudential policy (IMF 2012).

Thus, despite the role of push and pull factors in capital flows, in reality, individual economies use unilateral national policies. Capital-sending countries do whatever is needed (financial nationalism) regardless of spillover effects on other countries. Affected countries also take whatever national policy is necessary to assuage the impact. While it provides the rationale for policy coordination, in reality, there is no effective coordination. Although this is nothing new and should not seem unusual, the problem becomes serious when a unilateral policy is taken by the world's largest economy, because its policy repercussions will easily spread globally through massive capital flows and alter the landscape of global liquidity. The resulting exchange rate pressure in emerging markets forced frequent market

[2] In the 1990s alone, financial crises hit Europe (1992/1993), Mexico/Latin America (1994), Asia (1997), Eastern Europe and the Russian Federation (1998). Crisis contagion has also become more global and less regional, as evidenced by the recent global financial crisis. New technology and better information enable financial spillovers by reducing structural distance.

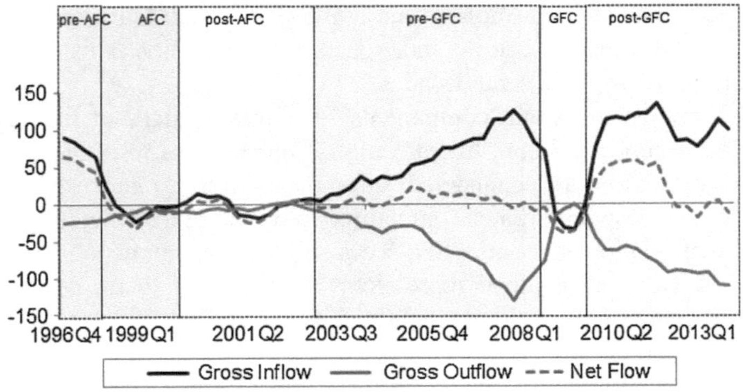

Fig. 5.1 Capital inflows and outflows—selected Asian economies. *AFC* Asian financial crisis; *GFC* global financial crisis. *Note* Data include Indonesia, the Republic of Korea, the Philippines, and Thailand; based on a 4-quarter moving sum, inflows refers to bank flows from other investments in liabilities (assigned a positive value); outflows are from assets (assigned a negative value). *Source* Processed from *Balance of Payments Statistics* (*both BPM5 and BPM6*), International Monetary Fund

intervention to maintain trade competitiveness. Policy makers in emerging markets also struggle to minimize the risk of financial instability. As additional funds flow in, economic agents take on more risks. Banks are more willing to invest in risky financial assets when bank-led flows increase. They are also more willing to lend because currency appreciation bolsters borrower balance sheets.

The problem arises when changes in investor sentiment or other external shocks cause asset prices to fall and capital flows to reverse. Bank balance sheets will be adversely affected, loans disrupted, and the economy can suffer from a credit crunch. Some of these were faced by several Asian economies when European banks deleveraged and retrenched funds to strengthen their capital position.[3] The elevated risks in Asia stem from very large amounts of capital flows coming into the region, as discussed in Chaps. 2 and 4. The discussions point to one common feature: the size and volatility of these flows have increased since the global crisis, more than what preceded the 1997/1998 Asian financial crisis (Fig. 5.1). As also discussed in Chap. 2, among the four types of capital flows, debt- and bank-led flows are the most volatile. This poses challenges for financial stability. We discuss how this affects welfare next—particularly the income distribution among different households in recipient economies.

[3] In the Republic of Korea, each 1 % decline in external funding due to European bank deleveraging led to a 0.01 % decline in domestic credit by domestic banks (Jain-Chandra et al. 2013). This occurred despite the economy's relatively healthy foreign reserves, government efforts to provide foreign currency liquidity through bilateral and multilateral currency swap arrangements, and macroprudential measures that lowered domestic bank reliance on short-term wholesale funding.

5.2 How Capital Flows Affect Income Inequality

To understand better how capital inflows can worsen socioeconomic conditions, we need to have a clear conception on how the impact is transmitted, and under what conditions inflows will trigger the process. Only then, appropriate policies can be identified.[4]

Figure 5.2 depicts the link between financial development, product and factor market, trade, and household income. It is a summarized flowchart explaining the transmission mechanism from increased capital flows in the financial market block to rising unemployment in the product and factor market block, and worsening income inequality and poverty in the household income block.[5] The middle part of the flowchart represents the dynamics in goods and factor markets (real sector)—including trade (exports and imports)—while the left side captures the workings of financial markets. The interconnection between the two determines the resulting unemployment and the generated household incomes in the income block (right part of the flowchart). Considering the endogenous prices, the poverty line can also be derived endogenously. The nature of the link between financial sector and real sector will thus influence income inequality and poverty. But the interrelations among variables are complex and nonlinear.

The characteristics of the interrelations among blocks and variables are similar to those often captured in a computable general equilibrium (CGE) model. To further describe the flowchart in Fig. 5.2, the real sector establishes the income generation from **output** production, with a portion covering the **domestic market** and **exports**. Together with **imports**, those sold in the domestic market generate the total **supply of goods and services**. In both allocations, the substitution is imperfect (not costless).[6] The process that generates **output** production follows a standard input–output framework, where **value added** and **intermediate inputs** jointly determine the level of **output** production. Expanding production networks and supply chains—where the location of production is different from the economy where the intermediate inputs are produced—suggests the need to distinguish between **imported intermediate inputs** and **domestically produced intermediate inputs**. This distinction is important particularly for trade analysis in many emerging market economies where the import content of many export products is large. The dynamics of the use of imported inputs to produce exported goods, known as vertical specialization, reflects a new paradigm in the overall global production network, which has increased dramatically since the 1980s, especially in high-tech products

[4] The analysis in this section is largely taken from Azis (2014).

[5] Not shown in the figure are prices of quantity variables, the role of which is critical in determining, among others, the endogenous poverty line.

[6] In a standard CGE model, for example, the allocation between the domestic market and imports follows Armington's constant elasticity of substitution, while the allocation between domestic market and exports follows a constant elasticity of transformation.

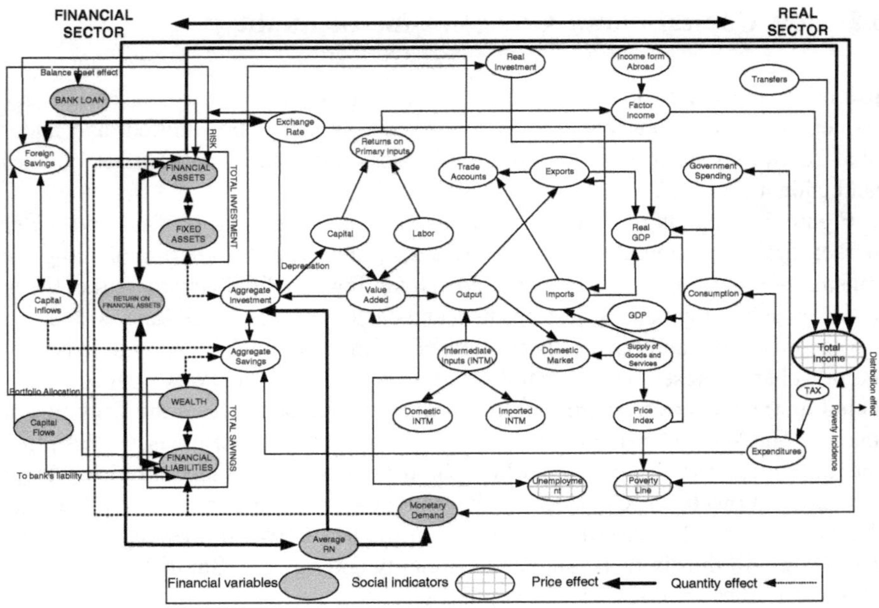

Fig. 5.2 Flowchart connecting real financial sector and income distribution. *Source* Modified from Azis (2014)

in emerging Asia (Hummels et al. 2001; Amador and Cabral 2009). It represents an important element of international trade.

To focus on the household incomes, we scrutinize the sources of income generation, both for primary and nonprimary incomes. The primary income is derived from the **value added**, the **returns on primary inputs** of **labor,** and **capital**. In turn, these **returns** generate **factor incomes** including **income from abroad**. However, **total income** consists of more than just factor income; it also includes transfers between agents/institutions. **Tax** payments that subtract and subsidies that add income are examples of these transfers, where size depends on the prevailing fiscal policy. Thus, income of different agents, including households, is influenced by both the level of economic activity and this nonfactor income.[7] The way subsidies are allocated can have significant impact on actual household income; typically, most subsidies go to low-income households.

But to capture the main essence of how capital flows affect household income distribution, we need to identify the income generation that originates in the financial sector. This is important because in reality the actual income received by the rich and urban-based households holding financial assets can be well above income accrued

[7] The effect of income level on macro variables works through the expenditure side. Together with government expenditure and net exports, real consumption reflects the size of agents' expenditure out of their disposable income. The latter is determined by income level.

by those who do not hold financial assets. Thus, even if factor incomes and transfers tend to be more equalized, earnings from these financial assets can worsen overall income inequality.

In a liberalized financial and capital account environment, rich urban-based households are better able to reap benefits from an expanding financial sector. During the "bubble" period following a surge in **capital inflows**, they benefit from the increased value of their **financial assets** as well as the income stream generated from those assets, regardless of what happens in the real economy. In many cases, this portion is larger than that generated from factor income. To the extent the financial sector often grows much faster than the real sector during a boom, the impact on income distribution can be predicted—the rich earn far more than the poor, and urban household income grows faster than rural income. Both of these exacerbate income inequality.

The increase in bank-led flows discussed in Chaps. 2 and 4 is first charted in **capital flows** at the bottom left of Fig. 5.2. Together with **bank loans**, these flows directly augment banks' **financial liabilities**.[8] This alters the rate of **return on financial assets** and financial returns received by asset holders (financial returns and income are linked). Financial assets also have a two-way relationship with the size and composition of different agents' assets. **Fixed assets** will be used directly for real sector **investment**, such as in buildings, machinery, and the like, while the rest—including **financial assets**—may move indirectly via financial markets; for example, funds from equity issuance are used for business investment. Along with **government spending**, **consumption** expenditure, **exports**, and **imports**, this **real investment** generates **real gross domestic product** (GDP).[9]

When there is an increase in **capital flows**, also captured by increased **foreign savings**, the **exchange rate** tends to appreciate. This is on top of the macrofinancial impact of the flows. The resulting **trade account** may thus worsen due to falling **exports** and increased **imports**. In reality, however, almost all emerging market economies with large capital inflows respond by imposing some sort of capital controls—either directly (through taxes or levies, for example) or indirectly (sterilized market intervention). This explains why net exports in some countries continue to grow despite increased capital inflows. When net exports shrink, the growth of **consumption** and **investment** can also offset the decline.

The resulting higher **real gross domestic product** fuels further financial sector growth either from strong fundamentals or simply market expectations. This further enhances rich household income along with **savings** or **wealth**, providing them with an additional income stream from financial returns. Note that changes in the exchange rate also cause some valuation effects: The local currency value of any assets denominated in foreign currencies will increase (decrease) when local currency appreciates (depreciates). If, through the portfolio allocation, the increased wealth is reinvested in financial instruments with lucrative returns, the

[8] As discussed in Chap. 4, lending is not only determined by the size of a bank's available funds, but also by changes in net worth and external finance premiums of both borrowers and lenders.

[9] Other financial variables can also affect aggregate economic activity through the money market.

financial assets and earnings of rich households increase yet again. This magnitude of the growth–inequality nexus is amplified through this feedback cycle.[10]

Thus, through this mechanism, we strongly argue that—in addition to standard factors like technology, globalization, education, and domestic institutions—the trend of rising inequality can be exacerbated by the noninclusive nature of financial sector growth.

To verify the above hypothesis, we use a financial computable general equilibrium (FCGE) model for one emerging Asian economy. Indonesia is selected for the following reasons. Like most emerging markets, the country's financial sector has been growing rapidly since financial liberalization began in the 1980s, and capital inflows after the global financial crisis also rose significantly. At the same time, Indonesia's income inequality has worsened. The model is the evolution of the original FCGE developed since late 1990s (Azis 1997). After several modifications and advancements, a more detailed household income distribution and poverty module was added in Azis (2009).[11] In the current version of the model, we delineate different types of capital inflows, distinguishing inflows that generate returns on financial assets directly from those of the foreign direct investment (FDI) type. How each of these flows enters the balance sheet of different agents and transmits to the rest of the economy is captured explicitly in the model (see again the flowchart in Fig. 5.2). The channel connecting financial flows and income distribution is specified in detail by dissecting the flows as they appear on agents' balance sheets, based on the type of income generated. Scrutinizing the role and detailed transmission within the financial sector allows us to analyze the dynamics of income earned from returns on financial assets held mostly by urban-based rich households.[12] On the banking side, the model also incorporates a credit channel component that includes the financial structure of lenders and borrowers in determining a bank's willingness to lend, and the amplified effect due to currency appreciation.

To simulate the model, we use Indonesia's Financial Social Accounting Matrix (FSAM) and more detailed capital flow data. Most parameters are calibrated on

---

[10] Aside from income inequality, poverty and unemployment are two other social indicators endogenously determined in the model. While unemployment is derived from the difference between labor demand and fixed labor supply, the aggregate variables in the real sector (total output (X), domestic demand (D), exports (E), imports (M), and total supply (Q)) are all determined along with their respective prices (PX, PD, PE, PM, and PQ). It is PQ that sets the overall price index. The poverty line (PL) can be derived from this. When PL is matched with the endogenously determined household income, the poverty level can be estimated.

[11] During its evolution, the model was applied to the dynamics of manufacturing sector in Azis (2000). It was then used to look at the impact of financial crisis on socioeconomic conditions in Azis (2003). Since then, the monetary block has been much improved and the model used to explain the disconnect between financial and real sector in Azis (2004). A more detailed breakdown of debt was made in Azis (2008), where debt maturity and debt reprofiling were specified based on this model version to analyze the debt sustainability issue.

[12] Due to space constraint, the detailed explanations of the model and simulation results are not shown (they are available upon request).

the actual data using the (nonlinear) model specifications, while others are econometrically estimated. The validity and the predictive power of the model are tested by plotting actual data on some exogenous variables.

The shock imposed on the model is capital flows intermediated through the banking sector (bank-led flows). In Chaps. 2 and 4, these flows are shown to dominate capital flows during phase one of global liquidity. For our purpose here, two scenarios are constructed: one where recipient banks increase risk by investing in financial assets, particularly securities and equity markets (labeled "Risky" in Fig. 5.3a–c), and the other where recipient banks spend the additional funds more prudently, by using them to strengthen more liquid and safe assets ("Nonrisky").

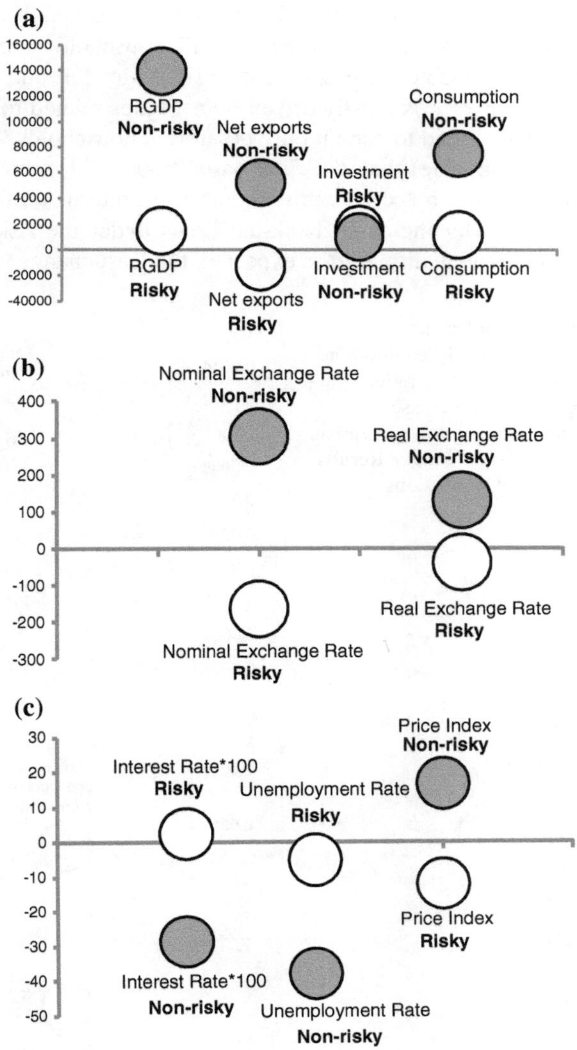

Fig. 5.3 **a** Impact of increased bank-led flows on aggregate demand. *RGDP* real gross domestic product. **b** Impact of increased bank-led flows on the exchange rate. **c** Impact of increased bank-led flows on prices, interest rates, and unemployment rate. *Source* Results of model simulations

In the first scenario, real GDP is only slightly above the baseline. So are investment and consumption. Given the augmented liquidity due to increased capital inflows, inflation and unemployment rates are lower. However, the trade sector suffers: Exports decrease and imports increase due to currency appreciation (Fig. 5.3a–c). Looking more closely, appreciation derives from higher interest rates, their level influenced by returns on financial assets. Because the issuance of financial assets increases under this scenario, prices will fall and yields rise, with interest rates also increasing. In the search for higher returns and yields, banks actively invest in these new assets instead of issuing more credit. This explains why the economy grows only slightly.

The effect on income distribution—whether measured by the disparity between rich and poor, or in terms of the rural/urban gap—is far more obvious. As shown in Fig. 5.4a, b, the inequality gets worse. Although the poverty line drops 1.2 % below the baseline, incomes for all household categories fall, despite growing GDP. Two factors are behind this: (i) Wages fall due to lower prices, and (ii) economic growth is mostly driven by activities related to the expanding financial sector. These tend to benefit only urban-rich households who depend far less on wages (factor income) than the rural-based poor. With more access to financial markets, the urban-rich accrue extra income from returns on the financial assets they hold. This is why increased bank-led flows under the risky behavior scenario worsen income inequality. And as expected, the least change is in financial income.

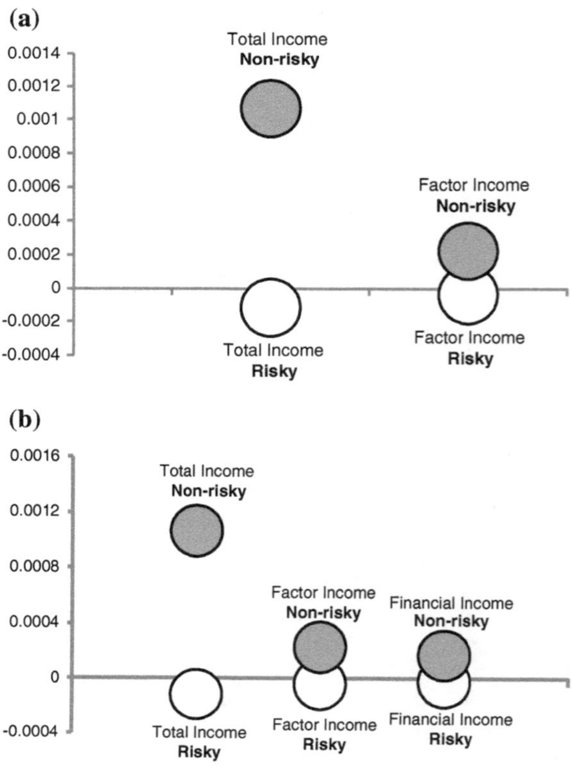

Fig. 5.4 **a** Impact of increased bank-led flows on poor/rich income ratio. **b** Impact of increased bank-led flows on rural/urban income ratio. *Source* Results of model simulations

In the "nonrisky" scenario, banks are assumed to behave prudently by extending more loans to productive sectors like manufacturing. As expected, the resulting real GDP is larger than under the "risky" scenario. The growth in investment and consumption is higher because of lower interest rates, and exports are also higher due to nominal and real exchange rate depreciation (see Fig. 5.3a, b). The unemployment rate is also much lower, though the price index is higher (see Fig. 5.3c). Thus, the macroeconomic impact is better when banks behave prudently.

Incomes of all household categories increase under this scenario. This is unlike in the previous "risky" scenario. As increased liquidity from bank-led flows is largely spent on loans to the real sector—not financial assets—output and hence factor incomes are higher. More importantly, from the income distribution perspective, the urban rich do not receive extra income from these assets. As a result, the overall income inequality narrows between rich and poor and between rural and urban households (see Fig. 5.4a, b).

Thus, the effect of increased bank-led flows on income distribution is clearly dependent on how a bank behaves. It is abundantly clear from the model simulation that the repercussions of increased bank-led flows depend on how banks react. The outcome is more favorable when banks act more prudently and do not take on increased risk. The problem is that there is no guarantee banks will behave that way. The discussions in Chaps. 2 and 4 clearly indicate that increased bank-led flows have been followed by increased bank investments in risky financial assets. Most financial institutions on the receiving end of capital inflows tend to take on more risk. As shown by the results of the model simulation, the aggregate demand and macroeconomic impact and the resulting income inequality are unfavorable. This suggests that particular measures are needed to influence the incentive–disincentive system for banks to act more prudently.

This is what macroprudential policy is expected to do. But the role of macroprudential policy is more than just reducing the risk of financial instability as discussed in Chap. 3. Its role in affecting socioeconomic development should also be assessed. Given such multiple objectives (stability in macrofinancial, microfinancial, and socioeconomic issues) and a whole range of policy options, which policy should be prioritized?

5.3 Prioritization for a Multi-objective Goal

In safeguarding the economy from the potential risks of bank-led flows, most emerging market economies refocused their policy on the asset and liability side of bank balance sheets.[13] This is a national policy taken unilaterally by each economy. But is this sufficient and effective enough to avoid the risk of the procyclicality discussed in previous chapters?

[13] On the asset side, aside from reducing loan-to-value ratios, efforts are made to contain excessive credit expansion and other risky investments. On the liability side, mitigating the increase of noncore liabilities through bank-led flows is critical because they can heighten risky bank behavior and increase leverage. See Azis and Shin (2013) and Forbes and Warnock (2012).

Given the sheer size of capital flows, would efforts to throw "some sand in the well-greased wheels of international finance" help reduce the potential risks of financial instability by limiting the risky behavior of economic agents? We have argued throughout that some sort of capital controls can help—in the form of direct quantitative controls such as imposing a macroprudential levy on bank-led flows (the role of such a levy as macroprudential policy and its application are discussed in the next chapter). But macroprudential policies at the national level may be inadequate to deal with large and volatile capital flows. Regional safety nets and cooperation can be a useful supplement, in particular to minimize the possibility and impact of financial spillovers and contagion.[14]

Because inflows and outflows are possible in an open capital account system, shouldn't we focus on how to balance outflows with inflows to limit the possibility of a crisis? Theoretically, capital outflows can be matched by retrenchment—returning foreign assets owned by domestic investors. But that works only if there are enough foreign assets. The size of these assets can only rise if capital outflows are encouraged before retrenchment is needed. This occurred, for example, in the People's Republic of China (PRC) when inflation began to rise in the mid-2000s. Since then, large capital inflows—especially FDI—and the increase in PRC surplus put strong pressure on the renminbi, forcing a roughly 6 % annual appreciation. In response, the central bank began to encourage capital outflows by the private sector and the newly established PRC Investment Corporation (CIC).[15] As a result, capital outflows from the PRC have indeed increased with low volatility (Fig. 5.5). While outflows from the Eurozone, the US, and Japan fell sharply during the global financial crisis, outflows from the PRC decreased only slightly. One of the reasons for the relative stability is the policy-driven nature of outflows, unlike the case of private flows, which almost exclusively search for better risk–return. More recently, however, non-CIC outflows increased significantly (Azis 2013).[16] Although detailed information on the breakdown of outflows is scarce, data from the balance of payments are suggestive. The share of equity and debt outflows by PRC residents and state-owned enterprises have surged along with bank lending abroad.[17] The resulting accumulation of net foreign assets fell

[14] For the status of Asia's regional financial safety nets, see Azis (2012).

[15] CIC is the second largest PRC investor overseas, ranking only behind the arm of the central bank that manages the economy's foreign exchange reserves. Attempts were also made by the central bank to share the burden with commercial banks by raising the required reserves in both local currency (sharing the burden of sterilization) and foreign currency (sharing the burden of intervention).

[16] As an example, in 2012 the PRC government approved a pilot program in Wenzhou, Zhejiang province, to allow city residents to privately invest overseas. Data on cross-border flows also show capital outflows to bond markets in other Asian economies—especially the Republic of Korea—has been rising.

[17] One estimate suggests resident lending abroad rose to $270 billion in 2012, double the amount in 2011. But the overall rise in overseas assets is due to investment by PRC financial institutions (IIF 2013).

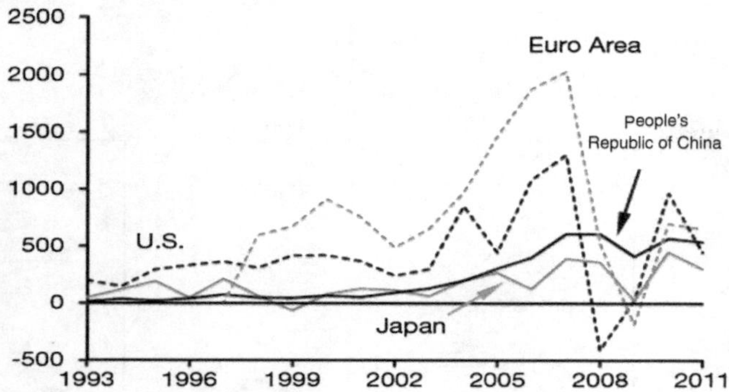

Fig. 5.5 Eurozone, Japan, United States (US), and People's Republic of China total outflows ($ billion). *Source* Institute of International Finance

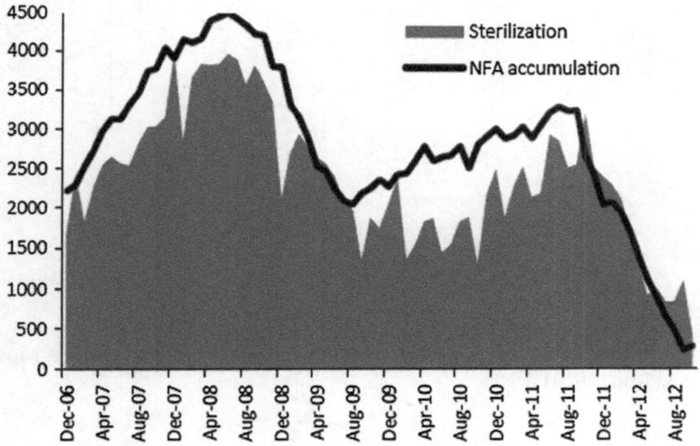

Fig. 5.6 Intervention and sterilization (CNY billion). *Source* Institute of International Finance

since mid-2011 (Fig. 5.6). By 2012, reserve accumulation declined to $85 billion (compared to $300 billion in 2011).

In prioritizing policy, therefore, three options are considered: (i) promote direct investment abroad, labeled "Encourage Outflows"; (ii) "Assign Levy" to noncore bank liabilities; and (iii) strengthen regional financial safety nets, "Reg Safety Nets." In Fig. 5.7, these three appear at the bottom of the hierarchy in each box that capture each component to consider. The logic of regional financial safety nets is to support domestic safety nets—as these remain far too inadequate—given the potential damage the unprecedented size and volatility of capital flows could

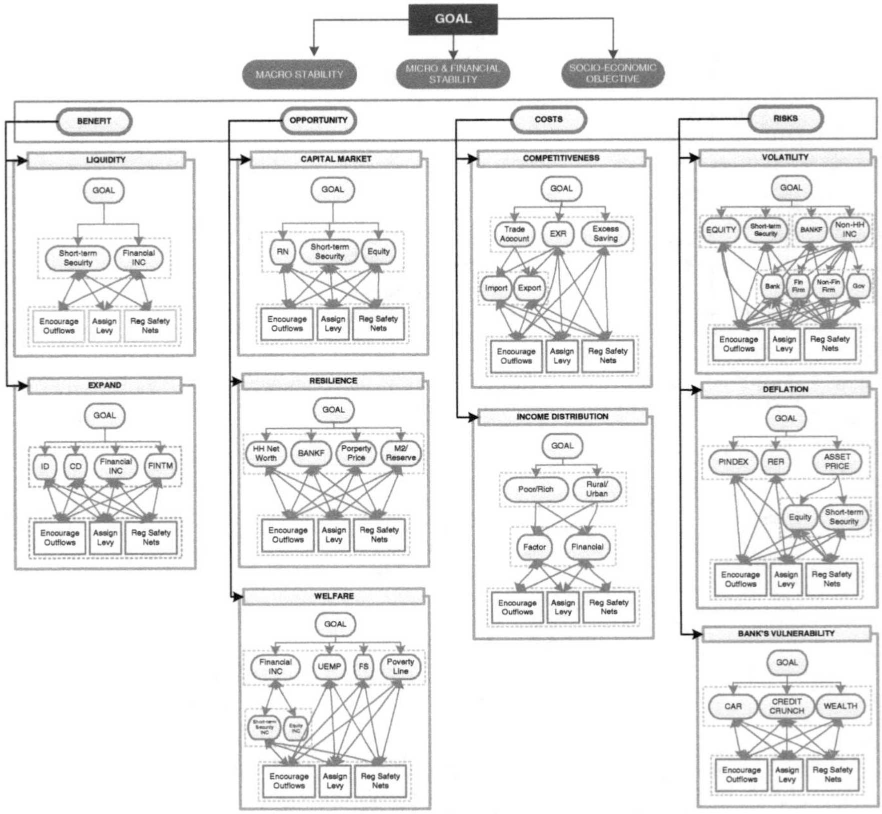

Fig. 5.7 Analytic network process (*ANP*) structure for policy options. *Source* Modified from Azis (2014) and Min (2014)

cause. The rationale for assigning a levy is to restrain rather than stop capital flows (see again the discussions in the previous chapters). Encouraging capital outflows helps maintain the stability of net flows. When capital tends to flow out in a crisis, during the boom-and-bust cycle, assets held abroad by domestic investors can act as a safeguard. They can provide a foreign asset buffer when markets become volatile. Indeed, the size of these ready-to-use foreign assets was important in some emerging market economies during the global financial crisis, the Republic of Korea being one example (Jain-Chandra et al. 2013).

So which policy works best? How do we prioritize the objectives, criteria, and the three policy options? Here, we use the analytic network process (ANP) to structure the model and quantify the weight of each model element (Fig. 5.7).[18]

---

[18] The figure is a slight modification of that in Azis (2014) and Min (2014), but the analysis follows the two references closely. For a detailed explanation of ANP, see Saaty (2005).

The strategic comparative goal is to achieve a balanced outcome of **MACROSTABILITY, MICROSTABILITY, and FINANCIAL STABILITY** and improved **SOCIOECONOMIC OBJECTIVES**, depicted at the top of Fig. 5.7. Each policy is weighted in terms of its relevance and contribution to **BENEFIT, OPPORTUNITY, COST, and RISK (BOCR)** that can be generated by increased bank-led flows. In the BENEFIT cluster, two sets of components are considered: (i) strengthen **LIQUIDITY** (the first box on the left of Fig. 5.7), through enhanced short-term securities and equity markets, along with boosted financial income, and (ii) allow investment, consumption, financial income, and imported intermediate inputs to **EXPAND** (the second box on the left of Fig. 5.7). Some beneficial impacts of increased bank-led flows, such as improved **CAPITAL MARKET**, and enhanced **RESILIENCE** may emerge only in the long run. Hence, they are listed under **OPPORTUNITY** cluster. Recipient countries can also improve overall **WELFARE**, after a certain period, if they take advantage and make good use of the increased capital inflows. The components connecting the **GOAL** and policies in Fig. 5.7 are most relevant and should be considered in prioritizing policies. For example, given an increase in bank-led flows, improvements in **WELFARE** can be fueled by a gradual increase in the financial income originating in short-term securities and equity earnings.

On the downside of bank-led flows, the short- and long-term costs (**COST** and **RISK**, respectively) are analyzed similarly, except that the priority ranking is based on "Which policy is most costly or risky?" when the following components are considered: **COMPETITIVENESS** and **INCOME DISTRIBUTION** under the COST cluster, and **VOLATILITY**, **DEFLATION**, and **BANK VULNERABILITY** under the RISK cluster. It is important to note that the reference for analyzing RISK is reversal of capital flows—as in many crisis episodes with a boom-and-bust cycle, the biggest risk in massive capital inflows is precisely that they can quickly reverse (procyclicality). However, one needs to distinguish this reversal from normal outflows from domestic investors. While useful in times of crisis—which is why one policy option is to encourage them—a capital flow reversal from investors pulling out will generate damaging capital "flight" (see again the distinction between capital "flight" and "retrenchment" discussed in Chap. 2).

The policies at the bottom of the network in Fig. 5.7 are weighted with respect to each component and subcomponent listed above them. For example, under BANK VULNERABILITY in the RISK cluster—where bank capital may deteriorate during a flow reversal—there is a risk that a bank's capital adequacy ratio (**CAR**) will deteriorate. The relevant question then is which of the three policies will likely create this risk (most risky)?

All arrows under each component in Fig. 5.7 point in two directions, implying a feedback effect for each influence from an element to the other elements below it. Thus, the structure in each box under each cluster forms a network. Taking the example of BANK VULNERABILITY in the RISK cluster again, a typical question is—"which risk is least likely to be resolved given a selected policy?" Applying pairwise comparisons, priority rankings for each feedback were made.

Table 5.1 ANP results for benefit (*B*), opportunity (*O*), cost (*C*), and risk (*R*)

	Ideals	Normals	Raw	Ranking
Benefit				
1. Encourage outflows	1	0.438129	0.858812	1
2. Assigning levies	0.994591	0.435759	0.854167	2
3. Reg safety nets	0.287844	0.126113	0.247204	3
Opportunity				
1. Encourage outflows	1	0.477338	0.826065	1
2. Assigning levies	0.712725	0.340211	0.588757	2
3. Reg safety nets	0.382225	0.182451	0.315742	3
Cost				
1. Encourage outflows	1	0.725513	1	1
2. Assigning levies	0.08878	0.064411	0.08878	3
3. Reg safety nets	0.289555	0.210076	0.289555	2
Risk				
1. Encourage outflows	1	0.488161	0.983803	1
2. Assigning levies	0.313358	0.152969	0.308283	3
3. Reg safety nets	0.735147	0.35887	0.72324	2

Source Results of ANP

The inputs used are a combination of the normalized quantitative data derived from the FCGE model simulations and analytical perceptions. The rankings based on the complex network structure are derived from the limiting super-matrix (see Appendix).

Table 5.1 shows the results of priority rankings for the three policies under the *BOCR*.[19] Thus, while to "Encourage Outflows" ranks highest in terms of its capacity to generate BENEFIT and OPPORTUNITY, the policy is also considered most costly and risky. For example, compared with "Assign Levy" and "Reg Safety Nets," "Encourage Outflows" will do the least in avoiding decreased competitiveness caused by the appreciation of real exchange rate (**RER**). On the RISK side, capital flow reversals may cause VOLATILITY in the **EQUITY** market. To "Encourage Outflows" will obviously make things worse.

[19] For example, under the BENEFIT scenario in Table 5.1, three eigenvectors are shown ("Ideals," "Normals," and "Raw"). While all three give the same ranking—encourage outflows being most preferred, followed by assigning levies, and regional financial safety nets (hence the ranking shown in the last column of Table 5.1)—the normalized eigenvector (0.4381; 0.4358; and 0.1261) under "Normal" with the sum equaling unity is the most often used. All numbers under the column "Benefit," "Opportunity," "Cost," and "Risk" in Table 5.2 show the normalized eigenvector.

Table 5.2 Overall results based on multiplicative and additive *BOCR*

ANP	Benefit	Opportunity	Cost	Risk	(*B***O*)/(*C***R*)	$bB + oO - cC - rR$	Ranking
	$b = 0.25$	$o = 0.25$	$c = 0.25$	$r = 0.25$			
Encourage outflows	0.438129	0.477338	0.725513	0.488161	0.590499767	−0.07455	3
Assign levy	0.435759	0.340211	0.064411	0.152969	15.04635304	0.1396	1
Reg safety nets	0.126113	0.182451	0.210076	0.35887	0.305205609	−0.0651	2

ANP	Benefit	Opportunity	Cost	Risk	(*B***O*)/(*C***R*)	$bB + oO - cC - rR$	Ranking
	$b = 0.25$	$o = 0.1$	$c = 0.35$	$r = 0.3$			
Encourage outflows	0.438129	0.477338	0.725513	0.488161	0.590499767	−0.2431	3
Assign levy	0.435759	0.340211	0.064411	0.152969	15.04635304	0.0745	1
Reg safety nets	0.126113	0.182451	0.210076	0.35887	0.305205609	−0.13141	2

ANP	Benefit	Opportunity	Cost	Risk	(*B***O*)/(*C***R*)	Ranking	$bB + oO - cC - rR$	Ranking
	$b = 0.35$	$o = 0.3$	$c = 0.25$	$r = 0.1$				
Encourage outflows	0.438129	0.477338	0.725513	0.488161	0.590499767	3	0.06635	2
Assign levy	0.435759	0.340211	0.064411	0.152969	15.04635304	1	0.22318	1
Reg safety nets	0.126113	0.182451	0.210076	0.35887	0.305205609	2	0.010469	3

Source Results of BOCR, based on ANP

Having calculated these priorities, the next step is to apply them to some BOCR formula. Two types are used here: (i) the multiplicative approach $(B^*O)/(C^*R)$ and (ii) the additive approach $(bB + oO - cC - rR)$.[20]

Table 5.2 lists the results. The upper panel equally ranks *BOCR*, with the last column showing the superiority of "Assign Levy." The middle and lower panels display the results of sensitivity analyses; the middle reflects a more subdued option, where COST and RISK clusters are weighted more than BENEFIT and OPPORTUNITY—the reverse case is shown in the bottom panel, representing a "buoyant" scenario. In either case, the highest preference for "Assign Levy" remains. Only the ranking of the other two policies is reversed when an additive approach is used. This suggests the superiority of placing a levy on bank-led flows is robust.

The policy analysis therefore suggests that during tranquil periods, capital outflows should be encouraged to help stabilize net flows in times of market turmoil. At the same time, this strengthens competitiveness as the exchange rate weakens. However, after considering both costs and risks, imposing a levy on bank-led flows works better. The resulting stable financial market feeds into the real economy, boosting factor income rather than returns on financial assets. This suggests it will also reduce inequality. Through sensitivity tests, the result is found to be robust. Clearly, taking a one-sided approach in evaluating policy alternatives—by neglecting the potential costs and risks of these policies—may produce a suboptimal result.

5.4 Appendix

The presence of feedback influences in a network model requires a large matrix—known as a super-matrix—that contains a set of submatrixes. The super-matrix captures the influence of elements in a network on other elements in that network. Denoting a cluster by C_h, $h = 1, \ldots m$, and assuming that it has n_h elements e_{h1}, e_{h2}, e_{h3} …, e_{hmh}, and laying out all clusters and all elements in each cluster both vertically (on the left) and horizontally (at the top), we have the super-matrix in Fig. 5.8.

The typical entry of this super-matrix is in Fig. 5.9.

The entries of submatrixes in W_{ij} are the ratio scales derived from paired comparisons performed on the elements within the clusters themselves,

[20] For the rationale of both, see Saaty and Vargas (2006).

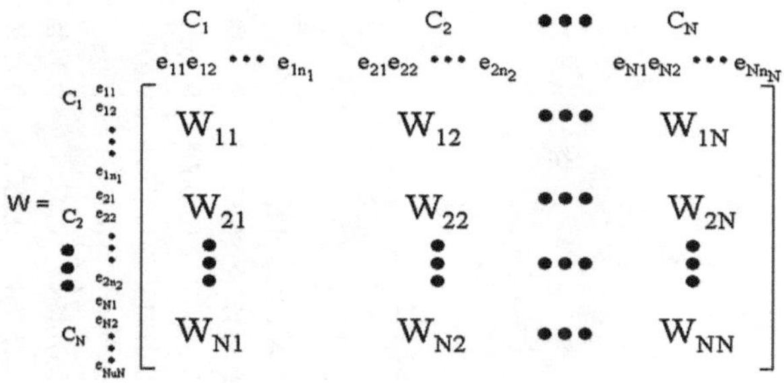

Fig. 5.8 Super-matrix of a network

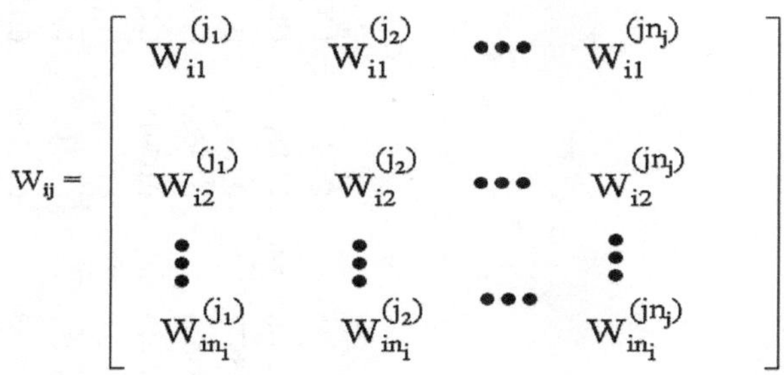

Fig. 5.9 Entries in super-matrix of a network

according to their influence on each element in another cluster (outer dependence) or elements in their own cluster (inner dependence). Judgments are elicited, from which ratio scales are derived. The resulting unweighted super-matrix is then transformed into a matrix where each column sums to unity to generate a stochastic super-matrix. The derived weights are used to weight the elements of the corresponding column blocks (cluster) of the super-matrix, resulting in a weighted super-matrix, which is also stochastic. The final ranking is derived from the limiting super-matrix, obtained by raising the stochastic super-matrix to large powers, in order to read off final priorities, in which all matrix columns are identical. Each gives the relative priorities of the elements from which the priorities of the elements in each cluster are normalized to one (the powers of the super-matrix do not converge unless it is stochastic, ensuring that its largest eigenvalue is one). Using the example of the EXPAND component under the BENEFIT cluster in Fig. 5.7, the resulting limiting super-matrix is displayed in Table 5.3.

Table 5.3 Limiting super-matrix

		Alternatives			Goal	EXPAND			
		Encourage outflows	Assign Levy	Reg safety nets	EXPAND	CD	FIN INC	FINTM	ID
Alternatives	Encourage outflows	0.18477	0.18477	0.18477	0.18477	0.18477	0.18477	0.18477	0.1848
	Assign levy	0.23605	0.23605	0.23605	0.23605	0.26305	0.23605	0.23605	0.2631
	Reg safety nets	0.07918	0.07918	0.07918	0.07918	0.07918	0.07918	0.07918	0.0792
Goal	EXPAND	0	0	0	0	0	0	0	0
EXPAND	CD	0.0745	0.0745	0.0745	0.0745	0.0745	0.0745	0.0745	0.0745
	FIN INC	0.15758	0.15758	0.15758	0.15758	0.15758	0.15758	0.15758	0.1576
	FINTM	0.13292	0.13292	0.13292	0.13292	0.13292	0.13292	0.13292	0.1329
	ID	0.135	0.135	0.135	0.135	0.135	0.135	0.135	0.135

Source Results of ANP

References

Amador J, Cabral S (2009) Vertical specialization across the world: a relative measure. North Am J Econ Finance 20:267–280
Azis IJ (1997) Impacts of economic reform on rural-urban welfare: a review of urban and regional development studies 3(Spring)
Azis IJ (2000) Non-linear general equilibrium impacts of financial crisis and manufacturing downfall. Developing Econ 2(December)
Azis IJ (2003) Modeling the repercussions of financial shock on socio-economic indicators. In: Ananta A (ed) The Indonesian crisis: a human development perspective. Institute of Southeast Asian Studies, Singapore
Azis IJ (2004) Modeling the disconnect between financial policy and real sector using the financial social accounting matrix as a data system: the case of Indonesia. In: Joseph C (ed) Banking disintermediation and its implication to: a theoretical view and country experiences. Bank Indonesia, Jakarta
Azis IJ (2008) Fiscal policy and workouts from debt crises: the case of Indonesia's domestic debt. IPD working paper, pp 1–25
Azis IJ (2009) Macro stability can be detrimental to Poverty. Econ Financ Indonesia 57(1):1–23
Azis IJ (2012) Asian regional financial safety nets? Don't hold your breath. Public Policy Review 8(3):321–340
Azis IJ (2013) Inadequate regional financial safety nets reflect complacency. ADBI working paper series 411
Azis IJ (2014) Integration, contagion, and income distribution. In: Nijkamp P et al (eds) Regional science matters. Springer, New York
Azis IJ, Shin HS (2013) How do global liquidity phases manifest themselves in Asia?. Asian Development Bank, Manila
Committee on International Economic Policy and Reform (2012) Banks and cross-border: policy challenges and regulatory responses. CIEPR, Washington DC
Forbes KJ, Warnock F (2012) Capital flow waves: surges, stops, flight, and retrenchment. J Int Econ 88(2):235–251
Institute of International Finance (2013) Capital Flows to Emerging Market Economies. IIF Research Notes(October)
International Monetary Fund (2012) The liberalization and management of: an institutional view. Washington DC
Hummels D, Ishii J, Yi K-M (2001) The nature and growth of vertical specialization in world trade. J Int Econ 54(1):75–96
Jain-Chandra S et al (2013) The impact of foreign bank on Korea. IMF working paper WP/13/101
Min HH (2014) The analysis of the link between capital flows and macroeconomic-financial-spatial income distribution indicators: combining financial CGE and perception models. Dissertation, Cornell University
Saaty TL (2005) Theory and applications of the analytic network process: decision making with benefits, opportunities, costs, and risks. RWS Publications, Pittsburgh
Saaty T, Vargas L (2006) Decision making with the analytic network process. Springer's international series

Chapter 6
Policy Implications

When global financial conditions affect domestic conditions, the institutional details of how they are transmitted matter. Designing and implementing policies that address these spillovers need to carefully take these channels into account. As the prolonged period of ample global liquidity starts to fade or comes to a close, a lively debate has begun over the impact capital flows have on the macroeconomic and financial conditions of recipient economies. Standard policy measures may need to be reviewed given the formidable role "supply-push" factors played, the growing significance of capital markets in determining monetary aggregates, and the specific circumstances including sociodevelopment challenges in each economy.

In this chapter, we discuss the range of policy options that can address the impact of global liquidity on domestic financial conditions. Monetary policy occupies an important place in the range of available policy options. But we argue that it may need to be complemented with macroprudential policies that account for financial vulnerability. We then outline the range of available policy options.

6.1 Tailoring Policies to Vulnerabilities

The three phases of global liquidity have somewhat different underlying mechanisms. But the policy challenges for recipient economies are equally significant during all three phases. For economies affected by the first two phases of global liquidity—and where economic fundamentals are relatively weak—the policy challenges in the third phase become even more daunting.

Macroprudential policy tools aim to mitigate the buildup of vulnerabilities to financial instability. For the reasons outlined in earlier chapters, the primary aim of macroprudential policy is to secure financial stability by leaning against permissive financial conditions (should they be deemed excessive) and to lean against excessive credit growth.

I.J. Azis and H.S. Shin, *Managing Elevated Risk*,
DOI 10.1007/978-981-287-284-5_6

However, the policy should be aimed at handling vulnerabilities, not banks. Many of the macroprudential policies discussed in this chapter are aimed at banks. But it is important to put policies in the broad context of capital market development. This is especially true in the second phase of global liquidity, when the transmission channel expanded from banks to nonbanks.

The role of asset managers in transmitting global liquidity during the second phase has become a major topic of discussion. Feroli et al. (2014) have provided some analytical background to the role asset managers play in amplifying the procyclical nature of international capital markets. Azis (2014) has also described how the behavior of fund managers when liquidity surges may be optimal privately but not socially. Policy makers have started to highlight this role as well—see, for instance, the speech by Haldane (2014), the Bank of England's Executive Director for Financial Stability.

To be sure, the 2008/2009 global financial crisis and the unwinding of the first phase of bank-led global liquidity involved much deleveraging. However, past experience does not imply future bouts of financial instability will operate similarly. The financial market's "taper tantrum" in 2013 and the renewed turbulence in early 2014 were associated with selling pressure in fixed-income mutual funds, especially those holding emerging market debt. Moreover, the outflows involved both retail and institutional investors (Feroli et al. 2014). The US Treasury's Office of Financial Research (OFR) highlighted just this risk in its 2013 Annual Report (OFR 2013). It said that "yield seeking capital flows across borders, driven by both external and domestic factors, have driven a decline in local [emerging market] bond yields. Markets for emerging market bonds have grown increasingly more sensitive to changes in US interest rates." Clearly, deteriorating growth prospects in important emerging market economies could have a meaningful impact on the global economy.

The bout of emerging market turbulence in early 2014 showed that financial instability need not be associated with the banking sector, at least directly. Insolvency and the problem of "Too Big To Fail" do not concern long-term asset management investors, as these institutions have little effective leverage and do not threaten insolvency the way banks or highly leveraged hedge funds do.

Nevertheless, the lack of leverage does not rule out a meaningful impact on the real economy through exchange rate, or asset price changes that dampen corporate investment and growth directly. When the local currency yield curve steepens and the domestic currency depreciates, the financial conditions facing households and firms are also affected, with direct knock-on effects on investment, consumption, and output. This will eventually influence the incomes of different households, although the resulting outcome of the influence on income inequality remains to be examined.

Asset managers' procyclical investment strategies may be derived from several underlying sources. Feroli et al. (2014) explore their concern for relative performance in amplifying market movements. If there are investor pressures to redeem fund products, then procyclical behavior is exacerbated. Chen et al. (2010) present evidence of mutually reinforcing redemption pressures in mutual fund flows, resembling the way bank depositors display run-like responses. More generally,

Vayanos and Woolley (2013) have shown how momentum and reversals result from small agency friction, even with exclusively long-term investors. These findings highlight the need to better understand the market-wide impact of traditional delegated investors.

6.2 Macroprudential Tools

Despite the wide-ranging sources of financial instability, those emanating from banks draw most attention, and rightly so. The experience of the first phase of global liquidity and the unwinding of bank excesses serve as a reminder of the importance of finding the right combination of micro- and macroprudential policy tools. Traditional solvency regulations based on minimum capital requirements are a key component of the policy mix. But microprudential tools need to be supplemented by macroprudential ones.

There are many ways to group macroprudential tools for banks. One useful way is to distinguish between (i) bank capital-oriented tools that limit loan growth through altering bank incentives, (ii) asset-side tools that limit bank loan growth directly, and (iii) liability-side tools that limit vulnerability to liquidity and currency mismatches.

6.2.1 Bank Capital-Oriented Tools

6.2.1.1 Capital Requirements that Adjust Over the Cycle

Bank management of balance sheets is inherently procyclical, as explained in Chap. 3. The rise in asset values that accompanies a boom results in higher capital buffers in financial institutions, supporting further lending in the context of an unchanging benchmark for capital adequacy. During a bust, the value of this capital can drop precipitously, possibly even necessitating a cut in lending.

Current capital requirements can therefore amplify the credit cycle, making a boom and bust more likely. However, capital requirements that lean against the credit or business cycle instead—rise with credit growth and fall when it contracts—can play an important role in promoting financial stability and reducing systemic risk.

We have already commented on some of the measurement issues associated with the implementation of countercyclical capital buffers. The framework envisaged in Basel III has focused on the ratio of credit growth to GDP. There are two preconditions for this to succeed. First, the quantitative signals that trigger actions must accurately reflect the features of policy makers' target (such as excessively loose lending conditions). Second, in implementing them, policy makers must be able to move decisively and in a timely manner to ward off the buildup of vulnerabilities. We have already commented on the first point in Chap. 3. Here, we focus on the second point.

If the trigger for adjusting countercyclical capital requirements is predicated on authorities' discretion and judgment, then market participants and other interested parties will ramp up the pressure. This political economy problem is similar to what central banks face when tightening monetary policy to head off a property boom, for example. As private sector participants—such as construction companies or property developers—benefit from the short-term boom, they can be expected to pressure policy makers or intensify lobbying. These problems will be more acute if there is controversy over the exact stage of the financial cycle or how conclusive the empirical evidence presented by policy makers is.

Thus, these two issues—the accuracy of quantitative indicators and political economy problems—are in fact very closely related. One of the disadvantages of the countercyclical capital buffer is that it relies on the triggering of additional capital requirements in response to quantitative signals. Although these quantitative measures are relatively straightforward in simple theoretical models, in practice, there may be considerable challenges in their smooth and decisive implementation.

6.2.1.2 Forward-Looking Provisioning

Forward-looking provisioning requires the buildup of a loss-absorbing buffer at the time the loan is made—it shares similarities with the countercyclical capital buffer. However, there is a key difference between provisioning and equity in accounting treatment. The forward-looking provision is not counted as bank capital and hence is less likely to influence bank—which targets a specific return on equity. To the extent the bank uses its capital as the base for constructing its total balance sheet, the larger the equity base, the larger the balance sheet, and hence greater use of debt to finance assets. During a credit boom, the buildup of assets using debt financing will contribute to a buildup of vulnerabilities.

Accounting for the loss buffer as a provision rather than equity thus has a potentially crucial effect on bank behavior. By insisting on forward-looking provisioning, bank equity is reduced by the amount of the provision. During a boom, this reduction in bank capital can play an important role in "letting off steam" in the pressure to buildup the bank's balance sheet by removing some of its capital base.

For Spain's banking system, for example, forward-looking provisioning was important in cushioning the initial stages of the global financial crisis. But there is the question of whether building up loss-absorbing buffers by itself can be sufficient to cushion an economy when a major property bubble bursts, as Spain discovered during the recent financial crisis in Europe.

6.2.1.3 Leverage Caps

Caps on bank leverage can limit asset growth by tying total assets to bank equity. The rationale rests on the role bank capital plays as a constraint on new lending, rather than the Basel approach of using bank capital as a buffer against loss.

The main mechanism is the cost of bank equity, regarded by banks as more expensive than short-term debt. By requiring a larger equity base to fund the total size of the balance sheet, a regulator can slow asset growth.

There are some lessons from the Republic of Korea's use of leverage caps. In June 2010, Korean regulatory authorities introduced a new set of macroprudential regulations to mitigate excessive volatility of foreign capital flows. Specific policy measures included explicit ceilings on banks' foreign exchange derivative positions, regulations on FCY bank loans, and prudential regulations for improving financial institutions' foreign exchange risk management. These measures were intended to limit short-term FCY-denominated bank borrowings. They did so by requiring banks to put up more equity capital if they chose to increase volatile debt. The leverage cap on bank foreign exchange derivative positions had some success in limiting banks from hedging forward dollar positions with Korean won carry trades funded by short-term US dollar debt.

6.2.1.4 Loan-to-Value and Debt-Service-to-Income Caps

Asset-side tools act as direct brakes on bank asset growth, counteracting the superficial and temporary strength of individual bank capital ratios that are inflated due to temporarily depressed risk measures or to higher profitability during booms. Inevitably, there are tools that straddle alternative categories. For instance, central bank reserve requirements are an asset-side tool, but are more naturally discussed in connection with the noncore liabilities levy, as we do below. Here, we begin with loan-to-value (LTV) and debt-service-to-income (DTI) ratios. When monetary policy is constrained, administrative rules that limit bank lending such as caps on LTV and DTI ratios may be a useful complement to traditional tools for bank supervision. LTV regulations restrict the amount of a loan to a maximum percentage of the value of collateral. DTI caps operate by limiting a borrower's debt service costs to some fixed percentage of verified income.

Conceptually, it is useful to distinguish the two motivations for using LTV and DTI caps. The first is the consumer protection motive, where the intention is to protect household borrowers from taking on debt beyond what they can reasonably repay out of wage income. Under this motivation, LTV and DTI rules would be similar to those against predatory lending to uninformed households. Although this is an important topic for consumer protection policy, this is not the motivation relevant for macroprudential policy and is not discussed here.

Instead, the macroprudential rationale for imposing LTV and DTI caps is to limit bank lending to prevent both the buildup of noncore liabilities in funding these loans as well as to lean against eroding lending standards associated with rapid asset growth.

It is important to reiterate why conventional microprudential tools—such as minimum capital requirements—are insufficient to stem excessive asset growth. Minimum capital requirements rarely bite during a lending boom with high bank profitability and low measured risk.

Although LTV ratio caps are familiar tools, the use of DTI caps is less widespread. For the Republic of Korea and Asian economies such as Hong Kong, China, the use of DTI ratios has been an important supplementary tool for macroprudential purposes. DTI rules have the advantage that bank loan growth can be tied (at least loosely) to wage growth. Without this fundamental anchor, an LTV rule by itself is susceptible to the amplifying dynamics of a credit boom, which interacts with an increase in the value of collateral assets, for example, during a housing boom. Even though the LTV rule is in place, if house prices are rising sufficiently fast, the collateral value will rise as well, reducing the rule's effectiveness.

In the case of Hong Kong, China, DTI rules take on added significance due to the US dollar currency board, which prohibits an autonomous monetary policy. In this case, US monetary policy shocks are transmitted directly.

6.2.1.5 Loan-to-Deposit Caps

A cap on the loan-to-deposit ratio limits credit growth by tying it to growth in deposits. The Korean supervisory authority announced in December 2009 it would reintroduce the loan-to-deposit ratio regulation—which had been scrapped in November 1998 as a part of government deregulation efforts. The regulation mandates that the ratio of Korean won-denominated loans to won-denominated deposits should fall below 100 % by 2013. The rationale for this policy was to restrict loan growth by tying it to the deposit base.

With the deposit base as baseline, the definition of what qualifies as a deposit is strict. For instance, negotiable certificates of deposit are not included as a deposit in the denominator when computing the ratio. Although the requirement to meet the 100 % ceiling was set for the end of 2013, banks anticipated the eventual cap and began reducing their LTV ratios ahead of time.

However, one potential weakness is that the rule does not apply to Korean branches of foreign banks. As they supply a substantial amount of foreign exchange-denominated lending to Korean banks and firms, exempting foreign bank branches leaves a loophole. However, it could not have been easily plugged within the loan-to-deposit cap framework because foreign bank branches by their very nature mostly rely on funding from headquarters or from wholesale funding, rather than from local deposits.

For domestic banks, the loan-to-deposit ratio cap has two effects. First, it restrains excessive asset growth by tying loan growth to growth in deposits. Second, there is the direct effect on the growth of noncore liabilities and hence on the buildup of vulnerabilities that arise from the liability side of the balance sheet. In this respect, there are similarities between the loan-to-deposit cap and the levy on noncore liabilities.

Indeed, at the theoretical level, the loan-to-deposit cap can be seen as a special case of a noncore liabilities levy in which the tax rate is kinked—changing from zero to infinity at the threshold. However, the comparison with the noncore liabilities levy is more difficult as the loan-to-deposit cap applies only to loans, not to total assets or total exposure (including off-balance sheet exposure).

6.2.1.6 Levy on Noncore Liabilities

Liability-side tools address the buildup of vulnerabilities to liquidity and currency mismatches along with the underpricing of risk on global capital markets. A levy on noncore bank liabilities mitigates the buildup of systemic risk through currency or maturity mismatches. The levy works by counteracting the distortions to global funding conditions and the funding "supply push" by global banks.

As already discussed in earlier chapters, the stock of noncore liabilities reflects the stage of the financial cycle and the extent of underpricing risk in the financial system. A levy or tax on noncore liabilities can also mitigate pricing distortions that lead to excessive asset growth. The "financial stability contribution" recommended by the IMF to the G20 leaders in June 2010 is an example of this kind of corrective tax (IMF 2010).

A levy on noncore liabilities affects overall financial stability in several ways. First, the levy's base itself varies over the financial cycle. It bites hardest during the boom stage—when noncore liabilities are large—so the levy acts as automatic stabilizer even if the tax rate itself remains constant. Given the well-known political economy challenges facing regulators, this automatic stabilizer feature of the levy may have important advantages.

Second, the levy addresses financial vulnerability, leaving alone the essential financial function of channeling core funding from savers to borrowers. By only targeting noncore liabilities, the levy addresses externalities associated with excessive asset growth and systemic risk arising from bank interconnectedness. In other words, it addresses the "bubbly" element of bank liabilities, rather than the core liabilities of the banking system.

Third, targeting noncore liabilities can address the vulnerability of emerging economies with open capital accounts to sudden capital flow reversals due to bank deleveraging. Indeed, for many emerging economies, a levy on noncore liabilities could narrowly target just FCY-denominated liabilities.

The revenue raised by the levy is actually a secondary issue. Its main purpose is to align incentives. A good analogy is London's congestion charge—currently an £11.50 daily fee for driving a vehicle into central London. Its main purpose is to discourage drivers from bringing cars into central London, alleviating the externalities associated with traffic congestion. In the same way, the noncore liabilities bank levy should be seen primarily as a tool for aligning the incentives of banks closer to the social optimum. The secondary issue of revenue raised also benefits (perhaps for a market stabilization fund).

In December 2010, the Republic of Korea announced it would introduce a "Macroprudential Stability Levy" aimed at foreign exchange-denominated bank liabilities—for both domestic banks and foreign bank branches (the levy became effective August 2011). The rate for the Korean levy was set at 20 basis points for short-term foreign exchange-denominated liabilities of up to 1 year, falling to 5 basis points for liabilities exceeding 5 years. The levy proceeds are held in a special account under the Exchange Stabilization Account, managed by the finance ministry. The proceeds may be used as part of official foreign exchange reserves.

There is a key difference between the Republic of Korea's macroprudential levy and an outwardly similar levy introduced by the UK. In the UK case, the revenue goes into the government's general fiscal account and hence can be regarded as revenue raising. In contrast, the Korean levy is specifically used for financial stabilization.

6.2.1.7 Unremunerated Reserve Requirements

Perhaps, the best-known traditional form of capital control is an unremunerated reserve requirement (URR), where the central bank requires capital importers to deposit a specified fraction at the central bank. URRs are frequently used because the central bank runs both prudential policy and macroeconomic management. Also, the central bank normally has the discretion to use URR without the legislative approval required for other forms of capital controls, such as levies and taxes.

Most central banks impose some type of reserve requirement for deposits, especially when they fall under government-sponsored deposit insurance. The rationale for the reserve requirement here is that it acts as an implicit insurance premium paid by the bank in return for deposit insurance.

The macroprudential motivation for URRs is that it imposes an implicit tax on components of financial intermediary liabilities other than insured deposits and will likely have negative spillover effects. The introduction of a reserve requirement for nondeposit bank liabilities would raise the cost of nondeposit bank funding—thereby restraining their rapid growth during booms. In this case, the reserve requirement on nondeposit liabilities has a similar effect as a tax or levy on these liabilities, as we discuss below.

Examples of URRs are discussed comprehensively in an IMF note (Ostry et al. 2011). Chile established a URR in 1991 with a 20 % rate for periods varying by maturity. The rate was subsequently increased to 30 % for a 1 year deposit, regardless of maturity. However, the URR rate was reduced to zero in 1998.

Colombia set up a 40 % URR in 2007, where withdrawals within 6 months subject to a heavy penalty. The rate was increased to 50 % in May 2008. Also, to prevent the loophole of classifying some flows as foreign direct investment (FDI), a 2-year minimum requirement was implemented for inward FDI.

Although URR is an implicit tax on a balance sheet item, the implied tax rate itself will vary with the opportunity cost of funds and hence on the prevailing interest rate. The variability of the implicit tax rate necessitates some adjustment of reserve rates—raised high when interest rates are low. This is potentially a disadvantage relative to other measures.

Another issue is how to manage the central bank balance sheet as a consequence of URRs. The reserves would need to appear as a liability, with implications for fluctuations in the money supply in line with private sector use of nondeposit liabilities and the selection of counterpart assets on the central bank balance sheet.

Although not a core issue, there are also differences in revenue implications between a URR and a levy or tax. The reserve requirement raises revenue to the extent that the net income on assets held by the central bank and funded by the reserves would be positive. Hence, the bigger the interest spread between the asset and liability, the larger the income.

There is one advantage of URRs not shared by the levy—banks would have access to a liquid asset in case of a liquidity shortage or run on the financial market. In this respect, the URR would have some of the features of the Basel III liquidity requirement on banks (BCBS 2010).

However, a disadvantage of the reserve requirement is that it applies only to banks, rather than other financial institutions that use noncore liabilities. When faced with the possibility of arbitrage or with structural changes that shift intermediation from banks to market-based financial intermediaries, the URR would be less effective.

6.2.2 Relative Merits of URR Versus Levies/Taxes

The time delay between the announcement and effectivity of the Republic of Korea's Macroprudential Stability Levy offers useful lessons on the relative merits of URRs and levies or taxes. The legislative process required to pass a levy can considerably delay policy implementation. For the Republic of Korea, initial discussions began in February 2010, the announcement of the levy was in December 2010, and legislative hurdles were cleared in April 2011, while the levy became effective in August 2011.

With a rapidly changing external environment, such long delays make introducing a levy cumbersome and impractical as a first line of defense. Nevertheless, as in the Korean case, alternative measures that rely on existing legislation or other temporary measures can be used in the interim until the longer-term policy measures come into force.

In practice, the choice between URR and levies or taxes is driven by practical reasons for administrative expediency rather than matters of principle. Typically, the central bank is the best established policy institution with direct contact with financial markets and institutions. This long-established central bank status explains why URRs have been more prevalent than levies or taxes.

There are, however, exceptions. In Brazil, an inflow tax (IOF) was introduced in 1993, and legislation has been in effect since. Although the tax rate was zero during times the tax was not implemented, the infrastructure has been available for "dusting off" as circumstances demand.

Unlike a tax, a URR can usually be removed (or set to zero) more easily because the budget is not directly reliant on its revenues. For a similar reason, the macroprudential levy set by the Republic of Korea has been designed so the revenue has no budgetary implication, precisely to forestall potential political economy concerns.

6.2.3 Relationship with Other Stabilization Policies

An important consideration when formulating macroprudential policy is its link with broader macroeconomic stabilization policies, particularly monetary policy. In both advanced and emerging economies, monetary policy resonates broadly in securing financial stability.

Here, we focus on the specific macroprudential tools and their link to the debate on capital controls. To the extent, the external environment affecting the global banking system is a key determinant of the vulnerability of an economy to financial excess, considering macroprudential policies cannot easily be separated from the active debate on the merits of capital controls. The IMF has suggested the more neutral term "capital flow management," rather than the more emotive "capital controls" (IMF 2011).

Indeed, some macroprudential tools have many attributes similar to tools used in capital controls. For this reason, the IMF suggested classifying policies in terms of capital flow management (IMF 2011). It categorizes three types of macroprudential tools:

(i) Prudential tools have a primarily domestic focus and are not aimed at correcting capital flow distortions. Examples include LTV rules, caps on the loan-to-deposit ratio, and leverage caps, among others.
(ii) Currency-based tools are prudential measures that address vulnerabilities originating from distortions in the external environment—such as global liquidity conditions—but which restrict activity or impose costs based on currency distinctions rather than on investor residency. Examples include the Republic of Macroprudential Stability Levy on short-term foreign exchange-denominated bank liabilities. As discussed in Chap. 5, this is the most preferred kind of policy measure.
(iii) Residency-based tools are traditional capital controls that restrict activity or impose costs based on an investor's residence. Examples include administrative restrictions on ownership and taxes on portfolio inflows—the IOF currently imposed by Brazil.

Capital controls raise a complex set of issues concerning their ultimate objectives—whether the objective is to hold down the exchange rate or limit the total volume of inflows to slow exchange rate appreciation. These issues merit a separate discussion and do not concern us here. In this chapter, we focus exclusively impact of macroprudential policies on financial stability.

Capital controls have two broad rationales. The first is as a macroeconomic policy tool designed to lean against exchange rate appreciation. The second is as a prudential tool used for bolster financial stability. We do not have much to say about the first objective. The IMF's paper from its Strategy, Policy and Review Department discusses the variety of capital control tools and their rationale (IMF 2011).

The distinguishing feature of capital control tools is that they discriminate based on investor residence—whether the investor is domestic or foreign. Tools include inflow taxes, such as Brazil's IOF, as well as administrative measures that restrict or ban certain activities or investments that foreign investors can hold.

Although capital controls have been used to affect the pace of exchange rate appreciation, the evidence on their effectiveness remains controversial. However, there is much better evidence on the implications of capital controls on financial stability.

There is a strong empirical association between capital controls on the one hand and less severe forms of both (i) credit booms and (ii) foreign exchange borrowing on the other. From this perspective, the global financial crisis can be regarded as a natural experiment for the effectiveness of capital controls. There are also important implications for monetary policy autonomy.[1] Capital controls channel into financial stability through their effect on the composition of capital flows rather than their total amount. De Gregorio et al. (2000) and Cardenas and Barrera (1997) show capital controls are likely to tilt the composition of inflows away from short-term and debt claims toward longer-term claims with more benign financial stability implications. The survey paper by Magud et al. (2011) conducts a "meta-analysis" of existing survey literature on the effects of capital controls. Their results are based on a meta-analysis of 37 empirical studies, with four main findings. Capital controls (i) make monetary policy more independent; (ii) alter the composition of capital flows; and (iii) reduce real exchange rate pressures (although the evidence on the latter is more controversial). However, they (iv) do not reduce the volume of net flows (and hence, the current account balance).

To the extent capital controls have an effect on the composition of capital flows and the likely pace of currency appreciation that gives additional autonomy to monetary policy, both features appear to point to some role of capital controls within the broader macroprudential policy framework.

6.3 Financial Integration and Institutional Design

There are important variations in both legal form and funding model for a foreign-related bank. Subsidiarization is a distinction on its legal form—whether it is a domestically incorporated subsidiary or a branch of the parent bank—while the funding model is about the composition of the liability side of the balance sheet. It is important to distinguish whether the bank is funded mainly from local deposits or is substantially reliant on wholesale funding, either from the parent bank or from the wholesale funding market. We have already discussed how bank procyclicality appears to be intimately tied to its funding structure. When lending expands faster than its core deposits, the bank typically migrates to using noncore, wholesale funding to finance lending growth. As such, if foreign-owned banks rely

[1] For example, capital controls allowed the Chilean central bank to target a higher domestic interest rate over a 6–12 month period.

on wholesale funding for a substantial part of their lending, then procyclicality would be built into their balance sheet management.

For instance, foreign-owned banks in Central and Eastern Europe hold the legal form of subsidiaries. While these raised considerable local funding in their host economies, a key type of cross-border credit flow was interoffice funding channeled from their Western European parents. In this way, the operations of foreign-owned banks enabled a faster rate of credit growth than otherwise would have been possible. Conversely, fast repatriation of funding by the parent at the height of a crisis could create a credit crunch and endanger financial stability in the host economy. A major foreign bank's decision to contract lending in a host economy will lead to a slowdown in economic activity, which in turn may affect the decision of other foreign lenders—implying the host economy may find funding abruptly cut. Hence, in such a situation, there is a clear externality and a need for international cooperation.

As noted by the BIS (2010), many (non-Spanish) European banks use a centralized funding model in which US dollar funds are deployed globally through a centralized portfolio allocation decision. Some of the funds raised will thus flow to Europe, Asia, and Latin America—where global banks are active local lenders. At the margin, the shadow value of bank funding will be equalized across regions through the portfolio decisions of the global banks, so they become carriers of dollar liquidity across borders. However, the BIS report also notes that Spanish banks pursued an "arm's length" approach when managing subsidiaries. The fact that foreign-owned banks in Latin America have been owned by Spanish parent banks has translated into a funding strategy in which most of the funding has been domestic (local) deposit funding, backed up by more stringent local regulations than found in many advanced economies. In particular, Santander and BBVA subsidiaries are among the most important banks in the region.

Nevertheless, the large presence of Spanish banks has also been a source of concern for Latin American policy makers on the banking system's exposure to Europe's financial crisis. The "arm's length subsidiarization model" cushioned Latin America from the deleveraging shock of the global financial crisis.

A recent Inter-American Development Bank (IADB) report contains a detailed analysis of foreign banks in Latin America and their European bank exposure (IADB 2012) (Fig. 6.1).

As can be seen, Spanish banks are the most important holders of foreign claims, followed by the US. As a consequence, foreign claims are quite important and concentrated in Spanish banks, reaching about half of domestic credit in Peru (Fig. 6.2). Foreign banks have been an important source of financial deepening and "bancarization" of important segments of the population.

However, as already mentioned, most foreign claims are local claims (Fig. 6.3). Local funding in domestic currency reduces exposure of the Latin American banking system to foreign financing. It is interesting to note that some economies, such as Mexico—which has one of the largest levels of foreign claims with respect to domestic credit—is also an economy where international claims are only about a quarter of foreign claims. Therefore, despite the significant relevance of foreign banks in terms of credit, they are still financed primarily by local funds.

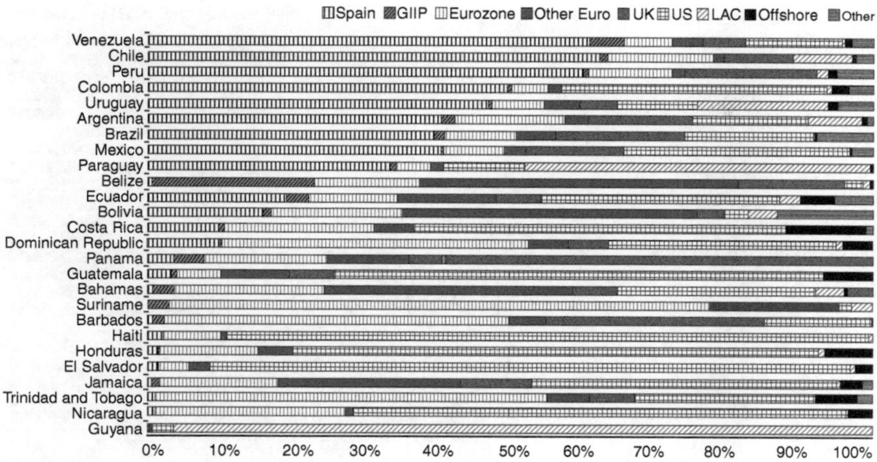

Fig. 6.1 Foreign claims of BIS-reporting Banks on Latin America and the Caribbean (as of 2011Q2). *GIIP* Greece, Italy, Ireland, and Portugal; *UK* United Kingdom; *US* United States; *LAC* Latin America and the Caribbean. *Source* IADB (2012), data from *Consolidated Banking Statistics* (immediate borrower basis), Bank for International Settlements (*BIS*)

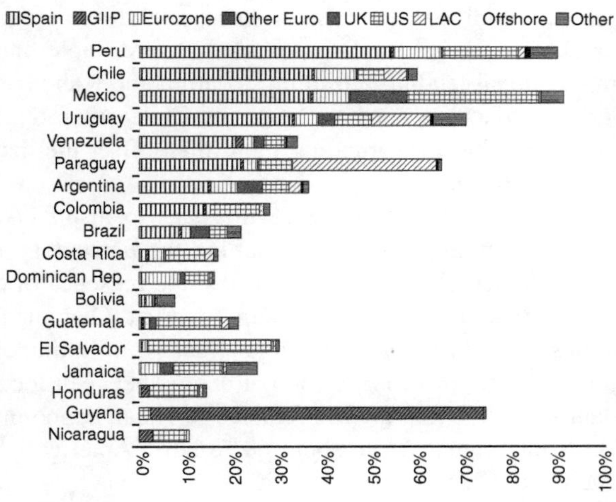

Fig. 6.2 Foreign Claims of BIS-reporting Banks on Latin America and the Caribbean (as of 2011Q2, % of total bank credit to domestic sector). *GIIP* Greece, Italy, Ireland, and Portugal; *UK* United Kingdom; *US* United States; *LAC* Latin America and the Caribbean. *Source* IADB (2012), data from *Consolidated Banking Statistics* (immediate borrower basis), Bank for International Settlements (*BIS*), and *International Financial Statistics*, International Monetary Fund

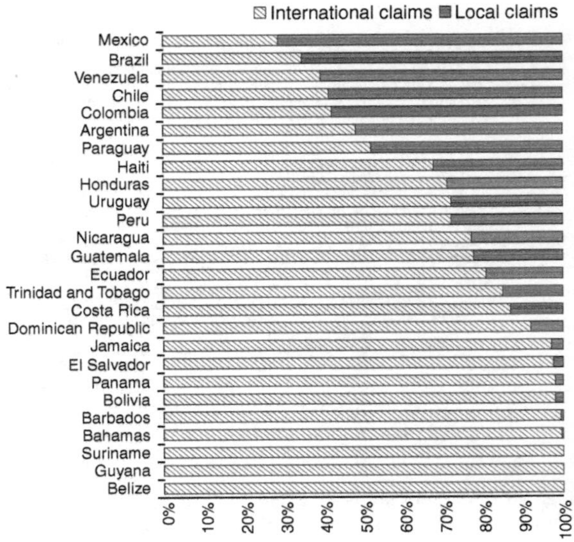

Fig. 6.3 Composition of foreign claims of BIS-reporting banks on Latin America and the Caribbean (as of 2011Q2). *Source* IADB (2012), data from *Consolidated Banking Statistics* (immediate borrower basis), Bank for International Settlements (*BIS*)

The proportion of local versus international claims implies differences in terms of banking procyclicality. While cross-border flows have significant comovements with global financial conditions (and Latin America did not escape this during the global financial crisis), local funding provides a more stable financing source. Indeed, while international lending fell in most Latin American economies during the 2008/2009 crisis, economies such as Brazil and Chile saw foreign claims actually increase, indicating that local funding more than offset the decline in cross-border lending (IADB 2012).

We can contrast the Latin American case with Asia. Spanish banks have far less exposure to counterparties in Asia. If we examine the percentage of total credit taken up by foreign claims of BIS-reporting banks, the presence of Spanish banks is far less visible in Asia compared with Latin America. Overall, foreign claims as a share of domestic credit are a much larger fraction in Latin America than in Asia. Examining the breakdown of the foreign claims between local and international claims, data also show the greater reliance of Asian economies on international rather than local claims. While about 60 % Latin America's foreign claims are local, this fraction declines to 40 % in Asia.

The evolution of cross-border and foreign claims did not prevent a reduction in domestic credit after the Lehman collapse, but the evidence suggests it was not necessarily triggered by especially procyclical foreign bank behavior. Indeed, the recession that followed the crisis came with a severe reduction in domestic credit. This was not simply due to tightened financial conditions on the side of lenders, but also a decline in credit demand.

Still, it is possible that in this banking model—based on multinational bank subsidiaries—there may still be strong local bank dependence on the economic health of the parent's financial system. Chile's experience illustrates how the local banking system can, over time, accommodate increased tensions in foreign funding. Chile's foreign debt from peripheral Europe—which includes Spain—has been declining sharply. Indeed, foreign bank affiliates have reduced lending from peripheral Europe from about 15 % in early 2010 to less than 3 % in 2012. There has been an important substitution from direct loans from peripheral Europe to bond issuance.

This evidence has a number of implications. Most importantly, Latin America—severely affected by international financial turbulence in the past—showed unusual resilience during the global financial crisis. High levels of indebtedness, weak banks, and currency mismatches were among the amplifying factors of previous bouts of global financial turbulence, especially in the 1980s and 1990s. This time has been notably different, despite its European bank exposure.

6.4 Policy Choices

What are the policy choices available? The Republic of Korea's experience makes it a good example to consider. It was hit hard by the 1997/1998 Asian financial crisis and was again severely affected by the financial turmoil after the Lehman Brothers failure in September 2008. In both cases, the source of vulnerability was the rapid buildup of short-term FCY bank liabilities. Recognizing this, the authorities introduced a series of macroprudential measures beginning in June 2010 to build resilience against capital flow reversals in the banking sector and the associated disruptions to domestic financial conditions. The first policy measure (announced in June 2010) was a leverage cap on the notional value of FCY derivatives contracts (encompassing currency swaps and forwards) that banks could maintain. For foreign bank branches, the leverage cap was set at 2.5 times their capital, while for domestic banks the cap was 50 % of their capital. Foreign banks could, in principle, increase their positions by allocating greater capital to their branches in the Republic of Korea, but the leverage cap lowers the return to capital for banks engaged in this segment of their business, thereby serving as a disincentive to expand their derivative positions.

The second component was the levy on the noncore liabilities of the banks mentioned earlier, the "Macroprudential Stability Levy" (see again the results of policy prioritization in Chap. 5). To recap, the levy consists of an annualized 20 basis point charge on nondeposit FCY liabilities with maturities up to 12 months. Lower rates are applied in a graduated manner to maturities over 1 year. The proceeds of the levy are paid into a special segregated account of foreign exchange reserves, rather than into the general revenue of the government. In this respect, the levy was designed from the outset as a tool for financial stability rather than for fiscal purposes. This contrasts with the outwardly similar bank levies introduced by several European economies after the global financial crisis. Also, by only targeting noncore liabilities, the levy was designed to address bank procyclicality, not the intermediation of core funding from savers to borrowers. The noncore liabilities levy was relatively novel compared with more standard capital-related or capital control tools such as URRs. Again, as mentioned earlier, it took 18 months from the time it was first mooted (February 2010) until effectivity (August 2011).

Bruno and Shin (2014) give a preliminary empirical assessment of the impact of the macroprudential measures. Their assessment is based on a panel study in which the Republic of Korea is one of 48 economies in a sample including both advanced and emerging economies. Their approach is to treat other economies as a comparison group and ask how the Republic of Korea's susceptibility to global supply-push factors in terms of capital flows compares with others during the sample period. Having obtained a benchmark for comparison from this cross-country panel study, they then ask whether the empirical relationship between the Republic of Korea and the comparison group changed in any noticeable way following the sequenced introduction of macroprudential measures beginning in June 2010.

They found that capital flows into the country did indeed become less sensitive to global supply-push factors after these measures were introduced. Interestingly, this change in sensitivity to global factors stands in contrast to other economies in the region. Clearly the experience in the Republic of Korea is the opposite of what happened in Australia, Indonesia, Malaysia, the Philippines, Thailand, and Viet Nam, where sensitivity to global factors actually increased after June 2010.

Short-term bank liabilities in the Republic of Korea continued to shrink after 2010 and were replaced by long-term liabilities in the form of long-term securities and loans (Fig. 6.4). The panel regression study allows for a more rigorous assessment of the policies by examining the country's experience compared with

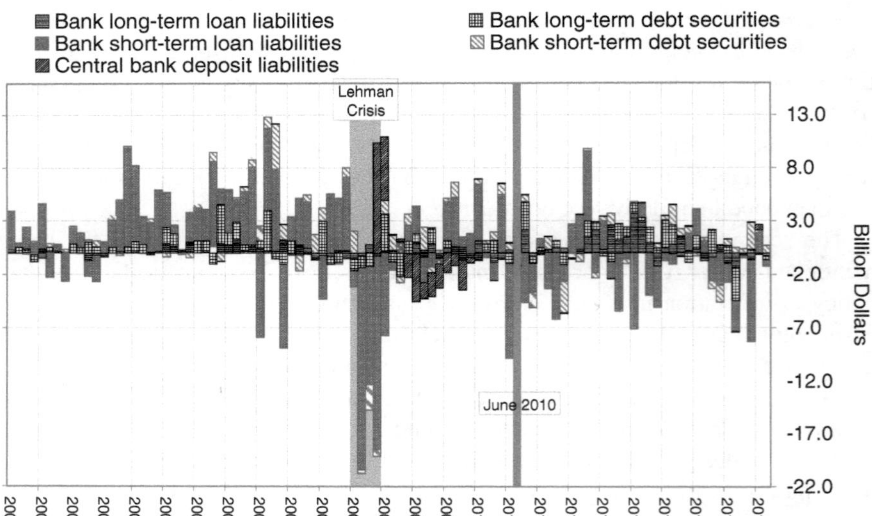

Fig. 6.4 Monthly capital flows to the banking sector in the Republic of Korea. *Source* Bank of Korea

other economies. The results confirm the impression that its sensitivity to global supply-push factors decreased after introducing macroprudential policies.

The measures used should be seen in the context of the broader debate on macroprudential policies. The evidence suggests that macroprudential measures aimed at enhancing financial stability may be effective in mitigating vulnerability to external financial shocks.

Although the above example pertains specifically to the Korean case, a similar measure can be considered in other emerging Asian economies where the banking sector experiences a surge in noncore liabilities. The key challenge for policy makers in general is to identify vulnerabilities. While each economy's circumstances may differ, broad principles can be useful. For economies with open capital markets, bank-led capital flows are key indicators of financial vulnerability. During a boom when bank assets are growing rapidly, the funding required outstrips the growth of the domestic deposit base. The gap is often filled by capital flows from international banks and is reflected in the growth of short-term FCY-denominated domestic bank liabilities. As such, short-term FCY bank liabilities can be viewed as being volatile noncore liabilities of the banking sector. For economies with relatively closed financial systems, where domestic banks do not have ready access to funding provided by the global banking system, a better approach would be to adapt existing conventional monetary aggregates to address financial stability. The key distinction is not how liquid the claims are, but rather who holds them. The distinction between household retail deposits and corporate bank deposits plays a particular important role.

Entering the third phase of global liquidity, emerging Asia faces a different set of policy challenges. With the reversal of capital flows, policy makers must deal with depreciating currencies, an economic slowdown, falling asset prices, and rising inflation. While this may look like a standard case, two circumstances distinguish it from a classical financial crisis. First, the trigger of capital outflows is a decrease in perceived risk in the US, not changes in emerging Asia's fundamentals. Second, capital markets in emerging Asia have grown steadily since the 1997/1998 crisis, meaning monetary aggregates are no longer influenced solely by monetary policy—the effects on the balance sheets of various institutions should be gauged more carefully.

Given the enormous size of the capital inflows, it has become more difficult to restore the equilibrium by using domestic economic policies when flows reverse. Dealing with structural issues that enhance efficiency and productivity can improve current accounts and fiscal balances. This is important, but requires medium-term policies. Countering the perception of relatively lower US market risk by raising domestic interest rates is far less effective compared with raising rates when outflows are driven by deteriorating domestic conditions. Only a very large increase in interest rates may be able to counter such outflows, but the risk of a recession can be huge. Confidence will likely deteriorate, fueling more capital outflows and thereby weakening the currency further—in a scene reminiscent of the 1997/1998 Asian financial crisis.

As capital markets in emerging Asia developed over the years, domestic agents and institutions have taken advantage by holding financial assets to safeguard returns.

Firms needing to secure long-term financing without risking a currency mismatch can raise funds through capital markets. Since the 1997/1998 crisis, more governments in Asia have also started to use local currency bond markets for budgetary purposes. Most of these securities are held by the banking sector. In this environment, the quality of a bank's balance sheet is influenced by mark-to-market prices or the value of financial assets it holds. Lower prices of bonds may help issuers to raise inexpensive fund, but lower value of bond holdings hurts the bank's net worth.

Figure 6.5 shows the trend of LCY bond holdings and bond issuance among corporates—including banks and nonbank financial institutions—in selected economies in emerging Asia. As argued in Azis and Shin (2013), in all cases, holdings exceed issuance, and in some economies, the gap is quite sizable. In Indonesia, for example, bond holdings are almost eight times bond issuance. If bond prices were to fall due to rising yields prompted by higher interest rates, the asset values on corporate balance sheets would likewise deteriorate. Some firms with strong fundamentals and ample liquidity may be able to withstand the pressure, but others,

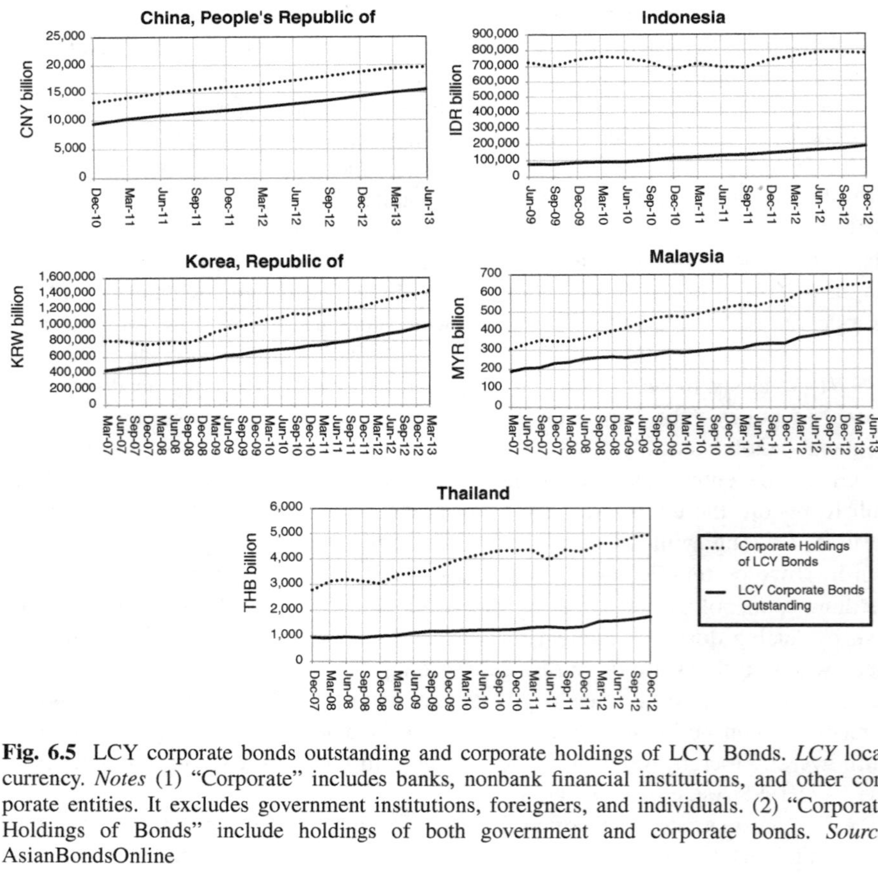

Fig. 6.5 LCY corporate bonds outstanding and corporate holdings of LCY Bonds. *LCY* local currency. *Notes* (1) "Corporate" includes banks, nonbank financial institutions, and other corporate entities. It excludes government institutions, foreigners, and individuals. (2) "Corporate Holdings of Bonds" include holdings of both government and corporate bonds. *Source* AsianBondsOnline

such as small banks, may be unable to do so. Banks without ample liquidity and a relatively large amount of nonperforming loans would be in a very difficult position. Thus, what started as a liquidity problem could easily become one of solvency.

As emerging Asia continues to expand its capital markets, defending the exchange rate by raising interest rates carries a bankruptcy risk for domestic firms. Allowing the currency to slide without much intervention will not only avoid insolvency, but also help preserve foreign exchange reserves. But if this path is taken, the economy still has to confront three risks: (i) imported inflation; (ii) rising foreign debt payments; and (iii) deteriorating market confidence due to a weakening currency. Of these three, only the last is a short-term challenge. The first two, while important, cannot be resolved immediately.

To deal with the problem of imported inflation, import dependence must be reduced, especially for exporters. But that requires structural change and medium-term policies in technology, education, the business environment, and investment incentives, among others. The problem of increased debt payment is linked to a debt structure in which the portion of FCY-denominated debt with short-term maturities is high—the double mismatch problem. Policies that discourage or even penalize this behavior are either ineffective or have only medium-term impact. More extreme policies—such as debt rescheduling or debt default—can backfire as investors may shun the market further.

That leaves us with the most unpredictable component—the confidence factor. Economic fundamentals can certainly play a role. Lowering current account and fiscal deficits, for example, will help restore investor confidence. Yet, this requires making changes in the production-cum-export structure and expanding the tax base, not a short-term solution. Cuts in imports of certain goods may help, but at the risk of falling investment and retaliation from trading partners. Allowing easier product exports—such as unprocessed materials—may quickly boost exports, but at the cost of stifling high value-added production-cum-exports, not to mention degrading the environment (resource depletion). Thus, the unknown aspect of market confidence is the most difficult to deal with. Regulators and the corporate sector also have a vital part to play, for example, by making mark-to-market accounting more flexible to prevent a downward spiral in asset prices.

Markets are neither to be fought with nor surrendered to. New policy packages taken by the authorities may be a necessary (albeit insufficient) condition for restoring market confidence. Fully restoring market confidence usually involves some measure of guarantees, direct financial resources, or establishing precautionary funds such as swap agreements and emergency external funds—including international and regional organizations, along with multilateral banks. Even with macroprudential policies, domestic financial safety nets may be inadequate in dealing with financial instability due to the size and volatility of capital flows. In such cases, regional financial safety nets can be useful. The Chiang Mai Initiative Multilateralized (CMIM) is an example within the ASEAN+3 framework. To the extent the power of an individual economy's safety nets is relatively limited—and in some cases nowhere near a match for damage enormous capital flows can cause—regional cooperation in providing financial safety nets can complement domestic efforts and existing bilateral swaps (Azis 2012). It can also minimize the probability of contagion, both intra-regional and external.

We have shown in Chap. 5 that when banks are getting more risk-taking, increased capital inflows can exacerbate the socioeconomic problems of unemployment, income inequality, and poverty. To ensure that banks behave more prudently, imposing a macroprudential policy is necessary. We have also shown that when socioeconomic objectives are included in the overall goal, a certain type of macroprudential tools can be more favorable than others. Given policy makers' strategic goal is to achieve the most balanced mix of (i) macroeconomic stability; (ii) micro and financial stability; and (iii) improved socioeconomic conditions, each available policy's relevance and contribution to attaining the right balance is assessed in terms of its benefits (*B*), the opportunities it can provide (*O*), as well as its associated costs (*C*) and risks (*R*). After considering a set of criteria for each component, three policy options are considered (i) promote direct investment abroad during the tranquil period; (ii) impose a levy on noncore bank liabilities; and (iii) strengthen regional financial safety nets. All three are important, but prioritizing them is necessary. Quantifying the weight of elements under each policy's BOCR, policy analysis suggests that encouraging outflows during tranquil periods is superior because it can help stabilize net flows in times of market turmoil, while at the same time strengthen competitiveness as the exchange rate weakens. But taking a one-sided approach by looking at only potential benefits and neglecting potential costs and risks is less than desirable. Indeed, by taking into account the costs and the risks of each alternative measure, encouraging capital outflows is not best. Imposing a levy on bank-led flows is most preferred. From a welfare perspective, the resulting financial market stability feeds into the real economy, boosting factor income rather than returns on financial assets. It suggests that imposing a levy as a macroprudential tool will not only reduce the risk of financial instability but also improve the socioeconomic conditions including income inequality.

References

Azis IJ (2012) Asian regional financial safety nets? Don't hold your breath. Public Policy Rev 8(3):321–340

Azis IJ (2014) Asia in a changing global liquidity: dancing with the system. Indonesian Q 42(2):80–98

Azis IJ, Shin HS (2013) How do global liquidity phases manifest themselves in Asia? Asian Development Bank, Manila

Bank for International Settlements (2010) Funding patterns and liquidity management of internationally active banks. CGFS papers 39

Basel Committee on Banking Supervision (2010) International regulatory framework for banks (Basel III). http://www.bis.org/bcbs/basel3.htm

Bruno V, Shin HS (2014) Assessing macroprudential policies: the case of South Korea. Scand J Econ 116(1):128–157

Cardenas M, Barrera F (1997) On the effectiveness of capital controls: the experience of Colombia during the 1990s. J Dev Econ 54(1):27–57

Chen Q, Goldstein I, Jiang W (2010) Payoff complementarities and financial fragility: evidence from mutual fund outflows. J Financ Econ 97(2):239–262

De Gregorio J, Edwards S, Valdés R (2000) Controls on capital inflows: do they work? J Dev Econ 63:59–83

Feroli M et al (2014) Market tantrums and monetary policy. US monetary policy forum report. http://papers.ssrn.com/sol3/papers.cfm?abstract_id=2409092

Haldane A (2014) Age of asset management. Speech, Bank of England. http://www.bankofengland.co.uk/publications/Pages/speeches/2014/723.aspx

Inter-American Development Bank (2012) The world of forking paths: Latin America and the Caribbean facing global economic risks. The Latin American and Caribbean macro report, Washington, DC

International Monetary Fund (2010) The IMF–FSB early warning exercise: design and methodological toolkit. http://www.imf.org/external/np/pp/eng/2010/090110.pdf

International Monetary Fund (2011) Recent experiences in managing capital inflows—cross-cutting themes and possible policy framework. http://www.imf.org/external/np/pp/eng/2011/021411a.pdf

Magud N, Reinhart C, Rogoff K (2011) Capital controls: myth and reality—a portfolio balance approach. National Bureau of Economic Research working papers 16805

Office of Financial Research (2013) Annual report to Congress. http://www.treasury.gov/initiatives/ofr/about/Documents/OFR_AnnualReport2013_FINAL_12-17-2013_Accessible.pdf

Ostry J et al (2011) Managing capital inflows: what tools to use? IMF staff discussion note SDN/11/06

Vayanos D, Woolley P (2013) An institutional theory of momentum and reversal. Rev Financ Stud 26:1087–1145

Index

I.J. Azis and H.S. Shin, *Managing Elevated Risk*,
DOI 10.1007/978-981-287-284-5

FSC
www.fsc.org
MIX
Papier | Fördert gute Waldnutzung
FSC® C083411

Kolibri 360 GmbH
Ferdinand-Jühlke-Straße 7
99095 Erfurt, Deutschland
produktsicherheit@kolibri360.de